A PRACTICAL GUIDE TO THE CONSTRUCTION REGULATIONS

A PRACTICAL GUIDE TO THE CONSTRUCTION REGULATIONS

Authors

Schorne Darlow

and

Johan Louw

LexisNexis Butterworths
Durban

Members of the LexisNexis Group worldwide

South Africa	LexisNexis Butterworths **DURBAN** 215 North Ridge Road, Morningside, 4001 **JOHANNESBURG** Grayston 66, 2 Norwich Close, Sandton, 2196 **CAPE TOWN** F10 Centurion Business Park, Milnerton, 7441 **PORT ELIZABETH** 7 Marlborough Street, Glendinningvale, 6001 **www.lexisnexis.co.za**
Argentina	LexisNexis Argentina, BUENOS AIRES
Australia	LexisNexis, CHATSWOOD, New South Wales
Austria	LexisNexis Verlag ARD Orac GmbH & Co KG, VIENNA
Canada	LexisNexis Butterworths, MARKHAM, Ontario
Chile	LexisNexis ChileLtda, SANTIAGO DE CHILE
Czech Republic	Nakladatelství Orac sro, PRAGUE
France	Editions du Juris-Classeur SA, PARIS
Hong Kong	LexisNexis Butterworths, HONG KONG
Hungary	HVG-Orac, BUDAPEST
India	LexisNexis Butterworths, NEW DELHI
Ireland	Butterworths (Ireland) Ltd, DUBLIN
Italy	Giuffrè Editore, MILAN
Malaysia	Malayan Law Journal Sdn Bhd, KUALA LUMPUR
New Zealand	LexisNexis Butterworths, WELLINGTON
Poland	Wydawnictwo Prawnicze LexisNexis, WARSAW
Singapore	LexisNexis Butterworths, SINGAPORE
Switzerland	Stämpfli Verlag AG, BERNE
United Kingdom	LexisNexis Butterworths Tolley, LONDON, WC2A
USA	LexisNexis, DAYTON, Ohio

ISBN 0 409 01257 2

Printed and bound by Interpak Books Pietermaritzburg

CONTENTS

Introduction

These regulations have been a long time in coming and when looking at incident statistics they can only be regarded as a necessary set of regulations. They are extremely long and cumbersome and will take great effort to ensure full compliance. It is clear that they are in line with the principle of self-regulation and responsibilities are placed on various parties to ensure that the next party is complying. This at the same time means that should a lower level contractor not be competent and not comply the legal liability will work upwards and a number of parties could be held legally accountable and liable. This is totally in line with the principle of section 37 of the Act.

The concept of placing the responsibility on those parties appointing a principal contractor and further down to the various levels of contractors in theory is good, the question, however, is whether there is sufficient expertise and knowledge to be able to manage what was intended by the legislature. For purposes of this book the actual regulation is reproduced in italics.

There are a number of onerous responsibilities placed on varies parties and again it is questionable as to whether such parties will be able to meet these duties.

A number of the regulations are repetition of what is already addressed in other regulations within the Occupational Health and Safety Act. This manner of repeating other regulations is not the normal practice and it must be questioned as to what the intention of the legislature was when drafting these regulations. Another question, which must be asked, is whether the authors of these regulations carefully thought through the consequences and the practicality of many aspects that have been included into these regulations. There are a number of areas of concern, which will be addressed under the commentary of each regulation.

Ladders have been left in the General Safety Regulations and have not been brought over to the new Construction Regulations. It would have made sense to have them under the Construction Regulations but there may be a reason that they were left behind. For purposes of this publication regulation 13A of the General Safety Regulations (which relates to ladders) has been included after the construction regulations.

Regulation 1: Definitions

In these Regulations any word or expression to which a meaning has been assigned in the Act shall have the meaning so assigned and, unless the context otherwise indicates—

***"agent"** means any person who acts as a representative for a client;*

***"angle of repose"** means the steepest angle of a surface at which a mass of loose or fragmented material will remain stationary in a pile on the surface, rather than sliding or crumbling away;*

***"batch plant"** means machinery, appliances or other similar devices that are assembled in such a manner so as to be able to mix materials in bulk for the purposes of using the mixed product for construction work;*

***"client"** means any person for whom construction work is performed;*

***"competent person"** means any person having the knowledge, training, experience and qualifications specific to the work or task being performed: Provided that where appropriate qualifications and training are registered in terms of the provisions of the South African Qualifications Authority Act, 1995 (Act No. 58 of 1995), these qualifications and training shall be deemed to be the required qualifications and training;*

"construction work" *means any work in connection with—*

(a) the erection, maintenance, alteration, renovation, repair, demolition or dismantling of or addition to a building or any similar structure;

(b) the installation, erection, dismantling or maintenance of a fixed plant where such work includes the risk of a person falling;

(c) the construction, maintenance, demolition or dismantling of any bridge, dam, canal, road, railway, runway, sewer or water reticulation system or any similar civil engineering structure; or

(d) the moving of earth, clearing of land, the making of an excavation, piling, or any similar type of work;

"construction vehicle" *means a vehicle used for means of conveyance for transporting persons or material or both such persons and material, as the case may be, both on and off the construction site for the purposes of performing construction work;*

"contractor" *means an employer, as defined in section 1 of the Act, who performs construction work and includes principal contractors;*

"design" *in relation to any structure includes drawings, calculations, design details and specifications;*

"designer" *means any of the following persons—*

(a) a person who prepares a design;

(b) a person who checks and approves a design;

(c) a person who arranges for any person at work under his control (including an employee of his, where he is the employer) to prepare a design, as well as;

(d) an architect or engineer contributing to, or having overall responsibility for the design;

(e) building services engineer designing details for fixed plant;

(f) surveyor specifying articles or drawing up specifications;

(g) contractor carrying out design work as part of a design and build project;

(h) temporary works engineer designing formwork and false work; and

(i) interior designer, shop-fitter and landscape architect;

"ergonomics" *means the application of scientific information concerning humans to the design of objects, systems and the environment for human use in order to optimize human well-being and overall system performance;*

"excavation work" *means the making of any man-made cavity, trench, pit or depression formed by cutting, digging or scooping;*

"explosive powered tool" *means a tool that is activated by an explosive charge and that is used for driving bolts, nails and similar objects for the purpose of providing fixing;*

"fall prevention equipment" *means equipment used to prevent persons from falling from an elevated position, including personal equipment, body harness, body belts, lanyards, lifelines or physical equipment, guardrails, screens, barricades, anchorages or similar equipment;*

"fall arrest equipment" *means equipment used to arrest the person in a fall from an elevated position, including personal equipment, body harness, lanyards, deceleration devices, lifelines or similar equipment, but excludes body belts;*

"fall protection plan" *means a documented plan, of all risks relating to working from an elevated position, considering the nature of work undertaken, and setting out the procedures and methods to be applied in order to eliminate the risk;*

"hazard identification" *means the identification and documenting of existing or expected hazards to the health and safety of persons, which are normally associated with the type of construction work being executed or to be executed;*

"health and safety file" *means a file, or other record in permanent form, containing the information required as contemplated in these regulations;*

"health and safety plan" *means a documented plan which addresses hazards identified and includes safe work procedures to mitigate, reduce or control the hazards identified;*

"health and safety specification" *means a documented specification of all health and safety requirements pertaining to the associated works on a construction site, so as to ensure the health and safety of persons;*

"material hoist" *means a hoist used to lower or raise material and equipment, and includes cantilevered platform hoists, mobile hoists, friction drive hoists, scaffold hoists, rack and pinion hoists and combination hoists;*

"medical certificate of fitness" *means a certificate valid for one year issued by an occupational health practitioner, issued in terms of these regulations, whom shall be registered with the Health Professions Council of South Africa;*

"method statement" *means a document detailing the key activities to be performed in order to reduce as reasonably as practicable the hazards identified in any risk assessment;*

"mobile plant" *means machinery, appliances or other similar devices that is able to move independently, for the purpose of performing construction work on the construction site;*

"National Building Regulations" *means the National Building Regulations made under section 17 (1) of the National Building Regulations and Building Standards Act, 1977 (Act No. 103 of 1977), and published under Government Notice No. R.1081 of 10 June 1988, as amended;*

"person day" *means one day for carrying out construction work by a person on a construction site for one normal working shift;*

"principal contractor" *means an employer, as defined in section 1 of the Act who performs construction work and is appointed by the client to be in overall control and management of a part of or the whole of a construction site;*

"professional engineer or professional certificated engineer" *means any person holding registration as either a Professional Engineer or Professional Certificated Engineer under the Engineering Profession Act, 2000 (Act No. 46 of 2000);*

"professional technologist" *means any person holding registration as a Professional Technologist under the Engineering Profession Act, 2000;*

"provincial director" *means the provincial director as defined in regulation 1 of the General Administrative Regulations under the Act;*

"risk assessment" *means a program to determine any risk associated with any hazard at a construction site, in order to identify the steps needed to be taken to remove, reduce or control such hazard;*

"roof apex height" *means the dimensional height in meters measured from the lowest ground level abutting any part of a building to the highest point of the roof;*

"SABS 085" *means the South African Bureau of Standards' Code of Practice entitled "The Design, Erection, Use and Inspection of Access Scaffolding";*

"SABS 0400" *means the South African Bureau of Standards' Code of Practice for the application of the National Building Regulations;*

"SABS EN 1808" *means the South African Bureau of Standards' Standard Specification entitled: "Safety requirements on suspended access equipment – Design calculations, stability criteria, construction-tests";*

"SABS 1903" *means the South African Bureau of Standards' Standard Front-end Specification entitled: "Safety requirements on suspended access equipment – Design calculations, stability criteria, construction- tests";*

"scaffold" *means any temporary elevated platform and supporting structure used for providing access to and supporting workmen or materials or both;*

"shoring" *means a structure such as a hydraulic, mechanical or timber/steel shoring system that supports the sides of an excavation and which is intended to prevent the cave-in or the collapse of the sides of an excavation, and* ***"shoring system"*** *has a corresponding meaning;*

"structure" *means—*

(a) any building, steel or reinforced concrete structure (not being a building), railway line or siding, bridge, waterworks, reservoir, pipe or pipeline, cable, sewer, sewage works, fixed vessels, road, drainage works, earthworks, dam, wall, mast, tower, tower crane, batching plants, pylon, surface and underground tanks, earth retaining structure or any structure designed to preserve or alter any natural feature, and any other similar structure;

(b) any formwork, false work, scaffold or other structure designed or used to provide support or means of access during construction work; or

(c) any fixed plant in respect of work which includes the installation, commissioning, decommissioning or dismantling and where any such work involves a risk of a person falling two meters or more;

"suspended scaffold" *means a working platform suspended from supports by means of one or more separate ropes from each support;*

"the Act" *means the Occupational Health and Safety Act, 1993 (Act No. 85 of 1993);*

"tunneling" *means the construction of any tunnel beneath the natural surface of the earth for a purpose other than the searching for or winning of a mineral.*

Regulation 2: Scope of application

(1) These Regulations, shall apply to any persons involved in construction work.

(2) The provisions of regulation 4 (1) (a) shall not be applicable where the construction work carried out is in relation to a single storey domestic building for a client who is going to reside in such building upon completion thereof.

(3) The provisions of regulations 4 (1) (a) and 5 (1), 5 (3) (a) and 5 (4) shall not be applicable where the construction work is in progress and more than fifty percent thereof has been completed at the date of promulgation of these regulations: Provided that an inspector may instruct accordingly that these Regulations shall be applicable.

It is quite clear that these regulations are applicable to all persons involved in construction work and to establish who this is one must study and understand the definition of construction work. The definition is self-explanatory and does not need to be explained, however, it should be noted that this definition is all encompassing and these regulations will therefore cover a very wide field of employers.

The provision of regulation 4 (1) (a) which is in relation to the health and safety specifications, which need to be given to the principal contractor, are specifically excluded for those persons who engage a principal contractor to build a single story domestic home. The important criteria, however, is that such person must reside in that domestic house after its completion. In other words regulation 4 (1) (a) would be applicable the case of domestic homes where the person is building domestic homes to sell. It is also interesting to note that the scope of application does not exclude the need for the principal contractor and contractors to carry over to the relevant party all the health and safety specifications that may be applicable.

In the case of construction work, which is more than fifty percent completed at the time of promulgation of these regulations, a number of requirements do not have to be met unless otherwise required by an inspector. These include the preparation of health and safety specifications by the client, a documented health and safety plan by the principal contractor, the need for the principal contractor to supply the contractor with applicable health and safety specifications and the need for the contractor to have a health and safety plan.

Regulation 3: Notification of construction work

(1) A principal contractor who intends to carry out any construction work shall—

(a) before carrying out that work, notify the provincial director in writing of the construction work if it includes—

(i) the demolition of a structure exceeding a height of 3 meters; or

(ii) the use of explosives to perform construction work; or

(iii) the dismantling of fixed plant at a height greater than 3 meters;

(b) before carrying out that work, notify the provincial director in writing when the construction work—

(i) exceeds 30 days or will involve more than 300 person days of construction work; and

(ii) includes excavation work deeper than 1 meter; or

(iii) includes working at a height greater than 3 meters above ground or a landing.

(2) The notification to the provincial director contemplated in subregulation (1) must be done on the form similar to Annexure A to these Regulations.

(3) A principal contractor shall ensure that a copy of the completed form contemplated in subregulation (2) is kept on site for inspection by an inspector, client, client's agent or employee.

The responsibility of notifying the provincial director of the Department of Labour of the intention of carrying out construction work lies solely with the principal contractor. Such contractor is required in terms of this regulation to prior to the commencement of the building work and it is merely notification and not application to carry out building work.

There are significant changes in respect to the notification of building work in comparison to the old requirements. You will notice that in regards to demolition work that if the height of the structure required being demolished exceeds three meters notification is required.

Also if explosives are used in any construction work notification is also required. This makes no sense at all because all this regulation merely requires notification and the Explosives Regulations require that permission be given by the chief inspector for all blasting activities. In other words, the requirements of the Explosives Regulations are much stricter than these and anyone doing construction requiring the use of explosives must not forget to ensure that they also meet the requirements of the Explosives Regulations.

Note that all notifications of construction work must be carried out in writing (refer to Annexure A of this book) and also include the notification of work that will exceed 30 days or 300 person days. Over and above this excavation work of more than 1 meter deep, note that in the old requirements it used to be more than 1.5 meters and an amount of more than 3 cubic meters had to be excavated. Strictly speaking, when interpreting this regulation now, it means that should one dig a hole of more than one meter to plant a pole, notification must first take place. This really appears to be totally unrealistic, however it is required and must be adhered to.

Notification is also required where construction work is to be carried out at a height of more than 3 meters above the ground or a landing. In the past the height criteria was more than 6 meters which was definitely more realistic.

In respect to these regulations a concern that must be expressed, is the fact that the Department of Labour is going to be flooded with notifications of construction work. In many instances the possibility exists that the inspectors time is going to be wasted on construction sites that have little or no risk attached to them, because of the nature of the work that is being carried out.

LCA Questions

1. Has the principal contractor notified the provincial director of:
    - the demolition of a structure exceeding 3 meters in height;
    - the use of explosives to perform construction work;
    - the dismantling of fixed plant at a height greater than 3 meters;
    - construction work exceeding 30 days or more than 300 person days;
    - excavation work exceeding 1 meter; or
    - construction work exceeding 3 meters above ground or a landing.
2. Has the notification of construction work been done in a form similar to Annexure A?

3. Has the principal contractor ensured that a copy of the notification form is available on site for inspection by an inspector?
4. Has the client appointed the principal contractor in writing for either the contract or part thereof?
5. Has the client ensured that the principal contractors health and safety plan has been implemented and maintained?
6. Has the client audited the principal contractor at least once a month?
7. Has the client stopped a contractor from carrying out any construction work that is a risk to the health and safety of any person?
8. Where changes have been brought about to the design or construction, has the client provided sufficient health and safety information and are appropriate resources made available to the principal contractor to execute the work safely?
9. Has the client ensured that every principal contractor is registered and in good standing with the compensation fund or a licensed compensation insurer prior to the commencement of work?
10. Has the client ensured that the principal contractor has allowed for a provision of costs in respect to health and safety in the tender?
11. Has the client discussed the health and safety plan with the principal contractor?
12. Has the client approved the principal contractors health and safety plan?
13. Has the client ensured that the principal contractors health and safety plan is available on request to an employee, inspector or contractor?
14. Has the client been satisfied that the principal contractor is competent and has the resources to carry out the construction work in a safe manner?
15. In those instances where the client has appointed an agent has the client ensured that such agent can be deemed to manage the interests of the client?

Regulation 4: Client

(1) A client shall be responsible for the following in order to ensure compliance with the provisions of the Act—

(a) to prepare health and safety specifications for the construction work, and provide any principal contractor who is making a bid or appointed to perform construction work for the client with the same;

(b) to promptly provide the principal contractor and his or her agent with any information which might affect the health and safety of any person at work carrying out construction work;

(c) to appoint each principal contractor in writing for the project or part thereof on a construction site;

(d) to take reasonable steps to ensure that each principal contractor's health and safety plan as determined in regulation 5 (1) is implemented and maintained on the construction site: Provided that the steps taken, shall include periodic audits at intervals mutually agreed upon between the client and principal contractor, but at least once every month;

(e) to stop any contractor from executing construction work, which is not in accordance with, the principal contractor's health and safety plan contemplated in regulation 5 (1) for the site or which poses a threat to the health and safety of persons;

(f) to ensure that where changes are brought about to the design or construction, sufficient health and safety information and appropriate resources are made available to the principal contractor to execute the work safely;

(g) to ensure that every principal contractor is registered and in good standing with the compensation fund or with a licensed compensation insurer prior to work commencing on site; and

(h) to ensure that potential principal contractors submitting tenders, have made provision for the cost of health and safety measures during the construction process.

(2) A client shall discuss and negotiate with the principal contractor the contents of the health and safety plan contemplated in regulation 5 (1) and thereafter finally approve the health and safety plan for implementation.

(3) A client shall ensure that a copy of the principal contractor's health and safety plan is available on request to an employee, inspector or contractor.

(4) No client shall appoint a principal contractor to perform construction work, unless the client is reasonably satisfied that the principal contractor which he or she intends to appoint has the necessary competencies and resources to carry out the work safely.

(5) A client may appoint an agent in writing to act as his or her representative and where such an appointment is made, the responsibilities as are imposed by these regulations upon a client, shall as far as reasonably practicable apply to the agent so appointed.

(6) No client shall appoint any person as an agent, unless the client is reasonably satisfied that the person he or she intends to appoint has the necessary competencies and resources to perform the duties imposed on a client by these regulations.

It must be noted with great interest that the client who is engaging a contractor to carry out construction work is now being bound by these regulations in a very serious manner. The client can no longer plead ignorance, as the legislature is clear in its intention to ensure that the client manages the contractor. The manner in which this regulation has been written binds the client to manage the principal contractor and it is in line with the requirements of section 37 of the Act in so far as the client must prove that he or she carried out their duties or he or she will be held liable for the actions of the appointed principal contractor.

There are a number of duties placed on the client, which are extremely onerous, and the first of these is the preparation of the health and safety specifications that must be provided to the principal contractor making a bid or appointed. Health and safety specifications are defined as documented specification pertaining to the work that is to be carried out so as to ensure that health and safety of persons. It would be interesting to know how many clients will be in a position to be able to meet this requirement. Most clients would employ a principal contractor for his expertise and would not really be in a position to prepare health and safety specifications as envisaged in this regulation. This would mean that the client would be forced to engage the necessary expertise to prepare such health and safety specifications in order to ensure that their interest are suitably protected. Note also that the client is required to provide any further information in respect to any changes that may brought about to the design or construction and is also responsible for the appropriate resources that may be required in terms of these changes, so that the work may be executed in a safe manner.

It would appear that the majority of clients would be in a position where they would have to appoint an agent who has to be suitable competent to meet the requirements of these regulations. This agent must be appointed in writing and such agent must be competent and have the necessary resources to be able to carry out his or her duties. The client is required to provide the agent and the principal contractor with any information, which might affect the health and safety of any person carrying out the construction work.

The client is required to appoint the principal contractor in writing for the project or part thereof. This means that there may well be more than one principal contractor on site. The important issue is that they must all be appointed in writing. Note that the client must ensure that the principal contractor is competent and has the necessary resources to carry out the construction work in a safe manner. The appointment of an incompetent contractor would be to the legal detriment of the client. This concept would also be applicable in the case of the appoint agent.

The client must also ensure that the principal contractor implements and maintains a health and safety plan. Again in this situation a certain amount of expertise would be required to carry out this task and again the client may have to rely on an agent to carry out this task. Here the client is required to carry out audits as agreed between the parties but such audit must be carried out at least monthly. It should be noted that this is not a five-minute task and depending on the size of the site it could be a costly affair. The client is required to stop the work if non-compliance is identified.

It would be practicable at this stage to discuss the health and safety plan, which is defined as a documented plan which addresses hazards identified and include safe working procedures to mitigate, reduce, or control the hazards identified. The definition does not really say much but it is envisaged that the health and safety plan is actually an implementation system to ensure the health and safety of person on site and to ensure legal compliance at all times. Such plan would have to go further than merely addressing the requirements of the Construction Regulations but would have to address the Occupational Health and Safety Act in its entirety. The client is required to discuss the health and safety plan with the principal contractor and here again the responsibility is placed on the client to approve the health and safety plan. This means that should the health and safety plan not be effective that the client could be held legally liable therefore. The client must also ensure that a copy of the health and safety plan is available on request by an inspector, an employee or a contractor.

An extremely important issue is that with respect to the Compensation of Occupational Injuries and Diseases Act. The client is required to ensure that the Principal Contractor is in good standing with the compensation fund or licensed compensation insurer. A valid letter of good standing must be produced to cover the period of the contract. Failure to do so could have serious legal and financial implications for the client. This must be done prior to commencement of the construction work.

The client is also responsible to ensure that the tender that is submitted addresses the cost in respect to health and safety issues. The client must at the same time ensure that the costs allocated for health and safety are realistic and that when carrying out the monthly audits also establish whether these costs are in fact being spent of health and safety issues and equipment. It makes no sense to merely ensure that a cost is allocated in the tender document but at the end of the day the money is not being spent at the detriment of the persons working on the construction site.

LCA Questions

1. Has the client prepared the health and safety specification for the construction work?
2. Has the client provide the principal contractors making a bid or who have been appointed with a copy of the health and safety specifications?
3. Has the client provided the principal contractor and his or her agent with any information which might affect the health and safety of any person carrying out the construction work?

Regulation 5: Principal contractor and contractor

(1) A principal contractor shall provide and demonstrate to the client a suitable and sufficiently documented health and safety plan, based on the client's documented health and safety specifications contemplated in regulation 4 (1) (a), which shall be applied from the date of commencement of and for the duration of the construction work.

(2) A principal contractor shall take reasonable steps as are necessary to ensure co-operation between all contractors to enable each of those contractors to comply with the provisions of these regulations.

(3) A principal contractor shall be responsible for the following in order to ensure compliance with the provisions of the Act—

(a) to provide any contractor who is making a bid or appointed to perform construction work for the principal contractor, with the relevant sections of the health and safety specifications contemplated in regulation 4 (1) (a) pertaining to the construction work which has to be performed;

(b) to appoint each contractor contemplated in paragraph (a) in writing for the part of the project on a construction site;

(c) to take reasonable steps to ensure that each contractor's health and safety plan contemplated in subregulation (4) is implemented and maintained on the construction site: Provided that the steps taken shall include periodic audits at intervals mutually agreed upon between the principal contractor and contractor(s), but at least once every month;

(d) to stop any contractor from executing construction work, which is not in accordance with, the principal contractor's and/or contractor's health and safety plan for the site or which poses a threat to the health and safety of persons;

(e) to ensure that where changes are brought about to the design and construction, sufficient health and safety information and appropriate resources are made available to the contractor to execute the work safely;

(f) to ensure that every contractor is registered and in good standing with the compensation fund or with a licensed compensation insurer prior to work commencing on site; and

(g) to ensure that potential contractors submitting tenders have made provision for the cost of health and safety measures during the construction process.

(4) A contractor shall provide and demonstrate to the principal contractor a suitable and sufficiently documented health and safety plan, based on the relevant sections of the principal contactor's health and safety specification contemplated in regulation 5 (3) (a) provided by the

principal contractor, which plan shall be applied from the date of commencement of and for the duration of the construction work.

(5) A principal contractor shall discuss and negotiate with the contractor the contents of the health and safety plan contemplated in subregulation (4), and shall finally approve that plan for implementation.

(6) A principal contractor shall ensure that a copy of his or her health and safety plan contemplated in subregulation (1), as well as the contractor's health and safety plan contemplated in subregulation (4), is available on request to an employee, inspector, contractor, client or client's agent.

(7) Every contractor shall ensure that a health and safety file, which shall include all documentation required in terms of the provisions of the Act and these Regulations, is opened and kept on site and made available to an inspector, client, clients agent or principal contractor upon request.

(8) A principal contractor shall hand over a consolidated health and safety file to the client upon completion of the construction work and shall, in addition to the documentation referred to in subregulation (7), include a record of all drawings, designs, materials used and other similar information concerning the completed structure.

(9) A principal contractor shall ensure that in addition to the documentation required in the health and safety file as determined in subregulations (7) and (8), a comprehensive and updated list of all the contractors on site accountable to the principal contractor, the agreements between the parties and the type of work being done are included and available.

(10) No principal contractor shall appoint a contractor to perform construction work unless the principal contractor is reasonably satisfied that the contractor he or she intends to appoint, has the necessary competencies and resources to perform the construction work safely.

(11) Where a contractor appoints another contractor to perform construction work, the responsibilities as determined in subregulations (2) to (6) that apply to the principal contractor shall apply to the contractor as if he or she were the principal contractor.

(12) No contractor shall appoint another contractor to perform construction work unless he or she is reasonably satisfied that the contractor he or she intends to appoint, has the necessary competencies and resources to perform the construction work safely.

(13) Contractors shall co-operate with the principal contractor as far as is necessary to enable each of them to comply with the provisions of the Act.

(14) Every contractor shall as far as is reasonably practicable, promptly provide the principal contractor with any information which might affect the health and safety of any person at work carrying out construction work or any person who might be affected by the work of such a person at work or which might justify a review of the health and safety plan.

Here it stipulates that the principal contractor must provide and demonstrate to the client a suitable health and safety plan based on the health and safety specifications given by the client. The principals behind the health and safety plan were discussed in detail under the client above. The entire construction operation must be carried out in accordance with the health and safety plan that clearly means that generic health and safety plans will have to be avoided and each construction operation will have its own specific health and safety plan. The plan must be adhered to for the entire operation.

The principal contractor is given the task of managing all the contractors on site and to ensure that there is cooperation between all the parties involved. However, all contractors are also required to cooperate. This not only places onerous duties on the principal contractor, but it should also be noted that should a client not appoint a principal contractor who is competent and who has all the resources necessary, it may occur that a client could at the end of the day be held liable for the actions of the principal contractor or the principal contractor's failure to take action.

As is the case with the client the principal contractor must now further appoint all contractors reporting to him in writing and must provided them with the applicable health and safety specifications, ensure that each contractor has a relevant health and safety plan, which is implemented and maintained on the construction site. The principal contractor must carry out audits on the contractors as agreed but at least once a month. The principal contractor must stop any contractor should they not be adhering either to the principal contractors health and safety plan or their own.

If there are any changes to the design and construction the principal contractor must bring these changes to the notice of the contractors. Also with respect to tenders that are submitted specific provision must be made for the costs of health and safety issues.

All these requirements are then transferred down to the next level of contractor and then further should there be further lower levels of contractors until every contractor on site is being managed.

All contractors on site are required to maintain a health and safety file in which all required documentation in terms of these regulations and also the Act must be filed. This safety file must be kept on site and must be available on request by an inspector, client's agent, client and principal contractor. The principal contractor is required to draw up a consolidated safety file and such file on completion of the construction work, shall be handed over to the client. The following is also to be included into the consolidated safety file, drawings, designs, materials used and other similar information.

The principal contractor is also required to draw up an updated list of all contractors on site who are accountable to that principal contractor, the agreements between the parties and the type of work being done are also to be included in this list.

Again as in the case with the client the principal contractor has to ensure that all contractors that are appointed are in fact competent and have the necessary resources to carry out the work required. Also should a contractor appoint another contractor these competencies and resources must also be ensured. The principal contractor must also ensure that all contractors are in good standing with the compensation fund or licensed insurer and so too must any contractor appointing another contractor.

It is again worth mentioning the principle behind these regulations at this stage, and that is to ensure that every contractor on site will be managed by another contractor. Also the legal liability and responsibility is transferred upwards to the contractor making the appointment. This could mean that should a contractor at a lower level be incompetent and such incompetence results in an incident, everyone including the client could be held legally liable.

LCA Questions

1. Has the principal contractor provided a documented health and safety plan drawn up according to the health and safety specification provided by the client?
2. Has the health and safety plan been implemented on the construction site?
3. Has the principal contractor taken steps to ensure that there is cooperation between all the contractors in respect to compliance to these regulations?

4. Has the principal contractor provided all the contractors making a bid or appointed to perform construction work with the applicable health and safety specification provided by the client?
5. Has the principal contractor appointed all contractors in writing for that part of the construction work they are required to perform?
6. Has the principal contractor ensured that all the contractors health and safety plans have been implemented and maintained?
7. Does the principal contractor stop all work that is carried out which is not in line with the health and safety plan of the contractor or principal contractor?
8. Does the principal contractor audit the contractors according to a mutually agreed period but which shall be at least once a month?
9. Where changes have been brought about to the design or construction, has the principal contractor provided sufficient health and safety information and are appropriate resources made available to the contractor to execute the work safely?
10. Has the principal contractor ensured that every contractor is registered and in good standing with the compensation fund or a licensed compensation insurer prior to the commencement of work?
11. Has the client ensured that the principal contractor has allowed for a provision of costs in respect to health and safety in the tender?
12. Have all contractors provided for a sufficiently documented health and safety plan based on the relevant sections of the principal contractor's health and safety specifications?
13. Has the principal contractor discussed the health and safety plan with the contractors?
14. Has the principal contractor approved the contractors health and safety plan?
15. Has the principal contractor ensured that the contractors health and safety plan is available on request to an employee, inspector, contractor, client or client's agent?
16. Have all contractors opened a safety file in which all required documentation is kept and made available for an inspector, client, client agent or principal contractor?
17. On completion of the contraction work has the principal contractor handed over to the client a consolidated health and safety file, which shall include all documentation required in terms of the Act and regulations, include all records of drawings, designs, materials used and other similar information concerning the completed structure?
18. Has the principal contractor provided a comprehensive and updated list of all the contractors on site accountable to the principal contractor, the agreements between the parties and the type of work being done, to the client?
19. Has the principal contractor been satisfied that the contractors are competent and have the resources to carry out the construction work in a safe manner?
20. Have all contractors who have further appointed other contractors ensured that they meet the required as laid down for a principal contractor?
21. Have all contractors ensured that they are satisfied that that all contractors contracting to them are competent and have the resources to carry out the construction work in a safe manner?
22. Do all contractors cooperate with the principal contractor to ensure compliance with the provisions of the Act?
23. Have all contractors provided the principal contractor with all information that may affect the health and safety of any person because of construction work carried out by that contractor?

Regulation 6: Supervision of construction work

(1) The contractor shall appoint a full-time competent employee in writing as the construction supervisor, with the duty of supervising the construction work.

(2) The contractor may in writing appoint one or more competent employees to assist the appointed construction supervisor contemplated in subregulation (1), and every such employee shall, to the extent clearly defined by the contractor in the letter of appointment, have the same duties as the construction supervisor: Provided that the designation of any such employee shall not relieve the construction supervisor contemplated in subregulation (1) of any personal accountability for failing in his supervisory duties referred to in terms of this regulation.

(3) Where the contractor has not appointed an employee as referred to in subregulation (2), or, in the opinion of an inspector, not a sufficient number of such employees, that inspector may require the employer to appoint the number of employees indicated by the inspector, and the provisions of subregulation (2) shall apply in respect of those employees as if they had in the first instance been appointed under subregulation (2).

(4) No construction supervisor appointed in terms of subregulation (1) shall supervise any construction work on or in any construction site other than the site in respect of which he or she has been appointed: Provided that a sufficient number of competent employees have been appropriately designated under subregulation (2) on all the construction sites, the appointed construction supervisor may supervise more than one site.

(5) If, however, the construction supervisor appointed in terms of subregulation (1) for more than one construction site will not, in the opinion of an inspector, be able to supervise the works favourably, an inspector may require the contractor to appoint the required number of employees as contemplated in subregulation (2) to assist the appointed construction supervisor or instruct the contractor to appoint the construction supervisor who had been appointed in terms of subregulation (1) more appropriately.

(6) A contractor shall upon having considered the size of the project, the degree of dangers likely to be encountered or the accumulation of hazards or risks on the site, appoint a full-time or part-time construction safety officer in writing to assist in the control of all safety related aspects on the site: Provided that, where the question arises as to whether a construction safety officer is necessary, the decision of an inspector shall be decisive.

(7) The appointed construction safety officer as contemplated in subregulation (6) shall as far as is reasonably practicable be utilised to give input at the early design stage and where not appointed at this stage, he or she shall be given the opportunity to input into the health and safety plan when wanting to do so, and a record of such shall be kept in the health and safety file contemplated in regulation 5 (7).

(8) No contractor shall appoint a construction safety officer to assist in the control of safety related aspects on the site unless he or she is reasonably satisfied that the construction safety officer he or she intends to appoint, has the necessary competencies and resources to assist the contractor.

All the contractors are required to appoint in writing a full time competent person as the construction supervisor, with the duty of supervising the construction work that is being carried out. Assistant may also be appointed in writing to assist the construction supervisor. Although the legislature does not clearly stipulate these persons duties it is clear that as a competent person in terms of General Machinery Regulation 2(1) is not required on a construction site, that such appointments are intended to actually fulfil the role of a competent person. In other words they are required to ensure that at all times the requirements of the Construction Regulations and the rest of the Act are adhered too. The construction supervisor is only allowed to supervise the site for which he has been appointed and only if there are sufficient number of assistants may such a construction supervisor be appointed for more than one site. An inspector is empowered to required that assistant supervisors be appointed and can also required that more of such appointees be appointed, as can an inspector require that a construction supervisor may only supervise one site or for fewer sites than for which he has been appointed.

The legislature requires that should the construction site be of such size, also taking into consideration the type of dangers that exist and also the accumulation of risks and hazards on site, that a site construction safety officer be appointed. Although a number of duties are placed on such a person, the likelihood that one would see many of these persons being appointed in terms of this regulation are slim. The reason for this statement is that the legislature actually drafted this regulation in such broad terms that in actual fact no need be appointed to this position. This is an example of where the legislature should have been specific with respect to the condition that must be in place for such a person to be appointed.

Again the legislature puts in the terminology that such safety officer may not be appointed if not competent and without the necessary resources. It may be practical at this stage to discuss this frequent referral to competency in these regulations. Although "competent person" is defined the definition is not really that helpful and all persons required to appoint a "competent person" to a position would have to ensure that they would be able to prove they acted reasonably when establishing any persons competency. Competency is loosely referred to regularly in these regulations and this could be a problem at the end of the day, particularly if something goes wrong, because one must then be able to clearly stipulate what was used as a criteria when establishing such persons competency.

It is interesting to note that the legislature deemed it necessary to include the appointed construction safety officer in the early design stage and it would be interesting to know whether there are in fact many safety officers with the necessary expertise to give constructive input at this stage. It may have been more practicable to rather have placed an onus on the designers and engineers to familiarise themselves and undergo the necessary training in respect to the applicable health and safety requirements.

LCA Questions

1. Have all contractors appointed a full time employee in writing as the construction supervisor?
2. In those instances where assistant supervisors have been appointed have their responsibilities been clearly defined in their letters of appointment?
3. Where an inspector has required that further assistant supervisors be appointed have such appointments been made?
4. Does the construction supervisor only supervise one site, and if required to supervise more than one site, are a sufficient number of assistant supervisors appointed?
5. Taking into consideration the nature of the construction site and the risks attached has the contractor appointed a safety officer for that site?
6. Has the appointed health and safety officer given input at the design stage and if not appointed at that stage has he or she been given the opportunity to give input into the safety plan?

7. Has a record been kept on the input given by a safety officer?
8. Has the contractor ensured that the health and safety officer has the necessary competency and resources to assist the contractor?

Regulation 7: Risk assessment

(1) Every contractor performing construction work shall before the commencement of any construction work and during construction work, cause a risk assessment to be performed by a competent person appointed in writing and the risk assessment shall form part of the health and safety plan to be applied on the site and shall include at least—

(a) the identification of the risks and hazards to which persons may be exposed to;

(b) the analysis and evaluation of the risks and hazards identified;

(c) a documented plan of safe work procedures to mitigate, reduce or control the risks and hazards that have been identified;

(d) a monitoring plan; and

(e) a review plan.

(2) A contractor shall ensure that a copy of the risk assessment is available on site for inspection by an inspector, client, client's agent, contractor, employee, representative trade union, health and safety representative or any member of the health and safety committee.

(3) Every contractor shall consult with the health and safety committee or, if no health and safety committee exists, with a representative group of employees, on the development, monitoring and review of the risk assessment.

(4) A contractor shall ensure that all employees under his or her control are informed, instructed and trained by a competent person regarding any hazard and the related work procedures before any work commences, and thereafter at such times as may be determined in the risk assessment.

(5) A principal contractor shall ensure that all contractors are informed regarding any hazard as stipulated in the risk assessment before any work commences, and thereafter at such times as may be determined in the risk assessment.

(6) A contractor shall ensure that as far as is reasonably practicable, ergonomic related hazards are analyzed, evaluated and addressed in the risk assessment.

(7) Notwithstanding the requirements laid down in subregulation (4), no contractor shall allow or permit any employee or person to enter any site, unless such employee or person has undergone health and safety induction training pertaining to the hazards prevalent on the site at the time of entry.

(8) A contractor shall ensure that all visitors to a construction site undergo health and safety induction pertaining to the hazards prevalent on the site and shall be provided with the necessary personal protective equipment.

(9) Every employee on site shall—

(a) be in possession of proof of the health and safety induction training as determined in subregulation (7), issued by a competent person prior to the commencement of construction work; and

(b) carry the proof contemplated in paragraph (a) for the duration of that project or for the period that the employee will be on the construction site.

Before even discussing this regulation one must be aware of the fact that section 8 of the Act requires that risk assessments be carried out. The legislature obviously deemed it necessary to place further emphasis on the need for risk assessments to be carried out in respect to construction work.

This regulation requires that every contractor carrying out construction work to cause a risk assessment to be carried out before the commencement and during construction work. This means that a number of risk assessments will have to be carried out and that all contractors shall have to carry out a risk assessment in respect to the specific tasks that they are required to complete. This means that at any one time on a construction site that there may be numerous persons carrying out risk assessments.

An area of concern is the risk assessment that must be carried out prior to the commencement of work on a construction site. This is an on-plan risk assessment and is not that easy to carry out and in many cases serious hazards may be overlooked by an inexperienced person. The legislation also does not stipulate specific frequency of risk assessment and it would be recommended that a specific plan of action in this regard be drawn up and that the requirements of this plan be met.

The legislation also requires that a competent person be appointed to carry out the risk assessment. Here again we sit with the competency requirement and care must be taken to ensure that such appointed person is in fact competent to carry out the task as envisaged in terms of this regulation.

The risk assessment must be included into the health and safety plan and must include the following, identification of risks and hazards, analysis and evaluation of the risks and hazards identified, a documented plan of safe work procedures, a monitoring plan and a review plan. These stipulated requirements actually go much further than requiring a mere risk assessment, they require that you also manage that risk.

Copies of all the risk assessments that are carried out must be kept on site and be available for inspection by an inspector, client, client agent, contractors, employees, representative trade unions or any member of the health and safety committee.

The monitoring reviewing and development of the risk assessment must be in consultation with the health and safety committee and if there is no committee with a representative group of employees. This actually means that agreement must be reached between the parties. The contractor must ensure that all employees are trained again by a competent person in respect to the risks that have been identified and the precautionary measure that need to be taken to manage the identified risks. This training must be carried out before any work has been carried out.

The principal contractor has to ensure that all contractors are informed of the risks that have been identified before any work by the relevant contractor commences. All contractors must also ensure that the risk assessment also addresses ergonomic related hazards, that they are analysed and evaluated.

It also stipulates in these regulations that no person may enter a site unless they have undergone induction training pertaining to the hazards on site and this would also include an inspector. It will be very interesting as to how this is going to be managed as it is currently not being applied throughout industry in general because the question that must be asked is how practical is this going to be for short term visitors. All visitors must also be provided with the necessary personal protective equipment. All employees that have undergone induction training must be provided with and be in possession of proof of induction training and must carry such proof on them at all times. It is recommended that a laminated type identification card in this regard be issued. This must be read in conjunction with General Safety Regulation 2 (c).

LCA Questions

1. Have all the contractors appointed a person in writing who is competent, to carry out a risk assessment before any construction work is started?
2. Has the risk assessment formed part of the health and safety plan?
3. Do the risk assessments include at least the following:
   - identification of he risks and hazards;
   - analysis of the risks and hazards;
   - a documented plan of safe procedures to mitigate, reduce or control the risks and hazards;
   - a monitoring plan; and
   - a review plan.
4. Have all the contractors ensued tat there is a copy of the risk assessment on site for inspection by an inspector, client, client's agent contractor employee, representative trade union, health and safety representative or any member of the health and safety committee?
5. Have all contractors consulted with the health and safety committee or if no committee exists with a representative group of employees, on the development, monitoring and review of the risk assessment?
6. Have all the contractors informed, instructed and trained their employees regarding all hazards and work related procedures?
7. Was the person carrying out the training competent?
8. Has the principal contractor informed all contractors of the hazards identified in the risk assessment before any work has commenced and at such times that may be determined in the risk assessment?
9. Have all contractors ensured that all ergonomically related hazards are analysed, evaluated and addressed in the risk assessment?
10. Have all contractors ensured that all persons entering the premises are required to undergo induction training?
11. Are all employees that are on site in possession of a certificate of health and safety induction training?
12. Has all training been given by a competent person?

Regulation 8: Fall protection

(1) A contractor shall cause—

(a) the designation of a competent person, responsible for the preparation of a fall protection plan;

(b) the fall protection plan contemplated in paragraph (a) to be implemented, amended where and when necessary and maintained as required;

(c) steps to be taken in order to ensure the continued adherence to the fall protection plan.

(2) The fall protection plan contemplated in subregulation (1), shall include—

(a) a risk assessment of all work carried out from an elevated position which shall include the procedures and methods used to address all the risks identified per location;

(b) the processes for evaluation of the employees' physical and psychological fitness necessary to work at elevated positions and the records thereof;

(c) the programme for the training of employees working from elevated positions and records thereof; and

(d) the procedure addressing the inspection, testing and maintenance of all fall protection equipment.

(3) A contractor shall ensure that the construction supervisor appointed in terms of regulation 6 (1), is in possession of the most recently updated version of the fall protection plan.

(4) Notwithstanding the provisions of subregulations (1) and (2), the contractor shall ensure that—

(a) all unprotected openings in floors, edges, slabs, hatchways and stairways are adequately guarded, fenced or barricaded or that similar means are used to safeguard any person from falling through such openings;

(b) no person works in an elevated position, unless such work is performed safely as if working from a scaffold or ladder;

(c) notices are conspicuously placed at all openings where the possibility exists that a person might fall through such openings;

(d) fall prevention and fall arrest equipment is—

(i) suitable and of sufficient strength for the purpose or purposes for which it is being used having regard to the work being carried out and the load, including any person, it is intended to bear; and

(ii) securely attached to a structure or plant and the structure or plant and the means of attachment thereto is suitable and of sufficient strength and stability for the purpose of safely supporting the equipment and any person who is liable to fall;

(e) fall arrest equipment shall only be used where it is not reasonably practicable to use fall prevention equipment; and

(f) suitable and sufficient steps shall be taken to ensure, as far as is reasonably practicable, that in the event of a fall by any person, the fall arrest equipment or the surrounding environment does not cause injury to the person.

(5) Where roof work is being performed on a construction site, the contractor shall ensure that in addition to the requirements set out in subregulations (2) and (4), it is furthermore indicated in the fall protection plan—

(a) that the roof work has been properly planned;

(b) that the roof erectors are competent to carry out the work;

(c) that no employees are permitted to work on roofs during inclement weather conditions or if weather conditions are a hazard to the health and safety of the employees;

(d) *that prominent warning notices are to be placed where all covers to openings are not of sufficient strength to withstand any imposed loads and where fragile material exists;*

(e) *that the areas mentioned in paragraph (d) are to be barricaded off to prevent persons from entering;*

(f) *that suitable and sufficient platforms, coverings or other similar means of support have been provided to be used in such a way that the weight of any person passing across or working on or from fragile material is supported; and*

(g) *that there is suitable and sufficient guard-rails or barriers and toe-boards or other similar means of protection to prevent, so far as is reasonably practicable, the fall of any person, material or equipment.*

This is a regulation that has been long in coming when one considers the number of fatalities that occur because of people falling from heights. The main concern here is, however, whether contractors are going to be successful with its implementation. Also this regulation falls under the Construction Regulations, which by implication means that fall protection is only applicable in terms of construction work. Although the definition of construction work is all encompassing there are areas where fall protection should be applied and which do not fall into the ambit of construction work such as the cleaning of windows. It is strongly recommended that all employers no matter what task they may be carrying out should apply this regulation in terms of any elevated height work.

All contractors are required to designate a person who is competent to prepare a fall protection plan which when taking into consideration the definition of fall protection plan, will be a documented plan to address all risks attached to elevated height work, taking into consideration the nature of the work being carried out and setting out the procedures to eliminate the risks. Again as was the case in the safety plan such fall protection plan cannot merely be generic and must be specific to the task being carried out. The plan must be implemented and maintained at all times and discipline in this regard must at all times be maintained.

Before a fall arrestor plan can be drawn up a risk assessment must be carried out to identify all the risks tat must be addressed in the plan. Included into the plan must be the assessment of the employees required to carry out the work in terms of their physical and psychological fitness. This aspect of psychological fitness is a new issue that has never in the past been addressed and it will be interesting how such fitness will be established. This is a medical assessment and not merely a few questions that need to be asked bearing in mind that some people may be desperate for work and would therefore answer the questions in such a manner that they would qualify for the work and this is unacceptable. Records of this assessment must be included into the fall protection plan.

The employees required to carry out this work need to be trained and the records of their training must be included into the plan. The procedures addressing the inspection, testing and maintenance of the fall protection equipment must also be included into the plan.
An updated copy of the fall arrestor plan must be placed in the possession of the construction supervisor appointed in terms of regulation 6(1).

Included into this regulation is the need to ensure that all areas from which a person can fall or through which he can fall must be adequately protected. No person may work from an elevated height unless from a ladder or a scaffold or in such a position that such person will be as safe as if he were working from a ladder or scaffolding. Warning notices must be posted at all areas where person could fall.

Again as in the old General Safety regulations the legislature has failed to define what an elevated height is. This results in the question as to what must be considered to be an elevated height and here the rules in respect to interpretation of statutes must be applied. This means that these regulations must be read as a whole before any interpretation can be made and when doing this one finds under the notification of construction work that the legislature speaks of a height of 3 meters in terms of notification. Therefore it would be reasonable to assume that the legislature regarded 3 meters as a risk and that 3 meters can be considered as an elevated height. Therefore it would be reasonable to assume that a fall protection plan must be developed for all work carried out at 3 meters or higher.

All fall arrestor and fall prevention equipment must be suitable and of sufficient strength and be securely fastened to a structure or plant that is of suitable strength.

It is important to note that before fall arrest equipment may be used fall prevention equipment must first be made use of and only where it is impracticable to use fall prevention equipment may fall arrest equipment be used.

Over and above what is already required to be included into the fall arrestor plan a number of issues need to be further included in those instances where roof work is being carried out. These issues include the proper planning of the roof work, the competency of the persons required to erect the roof, that no work may be carried out in inclement weather, that prominent warning signs be posted in those areas where the roof is of insufficient strength to carry persons or loads, That these areas are barricaded, that there are suitable and sufficient platforms erected and that there are barriers and toe boards in place.

The issue that arises here and which is extremely difficult to comply to, is the barricading on the roof and it may take some serious ingenuity to meet these requirements as envisaged by the legislature.

LCA Questions

1. Have all applicable contractors designated a competent person to prepare a fall protection plan?
2. Has the fall protection plan been implemented and maintained?
3. Is discipline enforced in respect to the fall protection plan?
4. Does the fall protection plan include a risk assessment on elevated height work and the procedures and methods to address the risks?
5. Does the fall protection plan include the process for evaluating the employee's physical and psychological fitness to work at elevated heights?
6. Does the fall protection plan include the programme of training in respect to elevated height work?
7. Does the fall protection plan include the procedure addressing the inspection and maintenance of the fall protection equipment?
8. Are there records in place in respect to the fall protection plan?
9. Is the construction supervisor in possession of the latest fall protection plan?
10. Has the contractor ensure that all openings in floors, edges, slabs, hatchways and stairways are adequately protected?

11. Has the contractor ensured that all elevated height work is performed from a position as if working from a ladder or scaffold?
12. Has the contractor posted notices in a conspicuous place at opening through which a person could fall?
13. Has the contractor ensured that fall prevention and fall protection is suitable and of sufficient strength?
14. Has the contractor ensured that fall prevention and fall protection equipment is securely attached?
15. Has the contractor ensured that fall arrest equipment is only used where it is not reasonably practicable to use fall prevention equipment?
16. Has the contractor taken suitable and reasonable steps to prevent a person who may fall from being injured by the protection equipment or surrounding environment?
17. Where roof work is being performed on a construction site that the contractor ensure that additional requirements be indicated in the fall protection plan which must include at least the following:
    - that the roof work is properly planned;
    - that the roof erectors are competent;
    - that no work is permitted during inclement weather;
    - that prominent warning notices are placed at all covers to openings that cannot sustain the applicable weight;
    - that covers to openings that cannot sustain the applicable weight be barricaded off;
    - that suitable and sufficient platforms, coverings are provided to be used in such a manner that persons passing across or working from fragile material is supported; and
    - that there are sufficient guard rails or barriers and toe-boards to prevent the fall of any person, material or equipment?

Regulation 9: Structures

(1) A contractor shall ensure that—

(a) all reasonably practicable steps are taken to prevent the uncontrolled collapse of any new or existing structure or any part thereof, which may become unstable or is in a temporary state of weakness or instability due to the carrying out of construction work; and

(b) no structure or part of a structure is loaded in a manner which would render it unsafe.

(2) The designer of a structure shall—

(a) before the contract is put out to tender, make available to the client all relevant information about the design of the relevant structure that may affect the pricing of the construction work;

(b) inform the contractor in writing of any known or anticipated dangers or hazards relating to the construction work, and make available all relevant information required

for the safe execution of the work upon being designed or when the design is subsequently altered;

(c) *subject to the provisions of paragraph (a) and (b) ensure that the following information is included in a report and made available to the contractor—*

(i) *a geo-science technical report where appropriate;*

(ii) *the loading the structure is designed to withstand; and*

(iii) *the methods and sequence of construction process;*

(d) *not include anything in the design of the structure necessitating the use of dangerous procedures or materials hazardous to the health and safety of persons, which could be avoided by modifying the design or by substituting materials;*

(e) *take into account the hazards relating to any subsequent maintenance of the relevant structure and should make provision in the design for that work to be performed to minimize the risk;*

(f) *carry out sufficient inspections at appropriate times of the construction work involving the design of the relevant structure in order to ensure compliance with the design and a record of those inspections is to be kept on site;*

(g) *stop any contractor from executing any construction work which is not in accordance with the relevant design;*

(h) *conduct a final inspection of the completed structure prior to its commissioning to render it safe for commissioning and issue a completion certificate to the contractor; and*

(i) *ensure that during commissioning, cognisance is taken of ergonomic design principles in order to minimize ergonomic related hazards in all phases of the life cycle of a structure.*

(3) A contractor shall ensure that all drawings pertaining to the design of the relevant structure are kept on site and are available on request by an inspector, contractors, client, client's agent or employee.

(4) Any owner of a structure shall ensure that inspections of that structure upon completion are carried out periodically by competent persons in order to render the structure safe for continued use: Provided that the inspections are carried out at least once every six months for the first two years and thereafter yearly and records of such inspections are kept and made available to an inspector upon request.

(5) Any owner of a structure shall ensure that the structure upon completion is maintained in such a manner that the structure remains safe for continued use and such maintenance records shall be kept and made available to an inspector upon request.

It is quite obvious that this regulation has been brought about because of the many building collapses that have occurred over the past few years. There is a definite need for safety of structure or buildings to be managed. However, some of the requirements in this regulation may not really be practicable and they will be discussed in detail.

All contractors are required to ensure that they take reasonable steps to ensure that structure erected by themselves are safe and do not collapse and that the same principal is applied to existing structures that may be affected by any construction work that is being carried out. This is a very broad statement and merely attempts to ensure that due diligence is applied by the relevant contractor. The same concept is also applied in respect to the loading of any structure to ensure that overloading does not occur.

What is extremely pleasing to see is that the designer of structure is also being pulled into the net and this should have been done many years ago. Duties are now placed on the designer to ensure that the client is specifically informed in respect to any pricing that may affect the safety of the structure regarding its design. The designer must now not merely design a structure but must also ensure that during the design stage that he or she identifies all the hazards in respect to safety relating to the construction work because the designer now has a duty to inform the contractor in writing of all the known and anticipated hazards that may occur.

The designer is also required to ensure that where appropriate that a geo-science technical report be drawn up, that the safe loading of the structure is established and the methods and sequence of the construction, all be included into a report and made available to the contractor. It is going to be interesting as to how the designer is going to establish the sequence of the construction and this will have to be done together with the relevant contractor. Designers must be made aware of the fact that this responsibility lies with them and together with this comes the liability. Should a structure collapse after the promulgation of these regulations the designer is going to have to do a lot of sweet-talking and it is essential in order to avoid this that communication between the designer and the contractor is good and continuing.

The designer are going to have to do their homework in the future in order to ensure that there are no procedure used including materials hazardous to the health and safety of persons, in instances where alternative design or materials can be used to make the process safer.

The designer's responsibilities no longer stop at the construction stage or its completion, but continue in such a manner to ensure that after construction has been completed, that the maintenance of the structure is also considered and taken into account at the design stage. This means that should an incident occur after the completion of the structure due to poor design or due to the hazards not been contemplated at the design stage, the designer will be held liable. This concept is similar to the requirements of section 10 and 22 of the Act.

The designer is now in terms of the legislation required to be involved during the entire process of the construction of the structure and must carry out regular inspections to ensure compliance to the design at all stages. This is a duty placed on the designer and failure to do so whether established at a later stage will lead to legal sanction. The designer is required to carry out a final inspection of the structure on completion and must then issue a certificate to the contractor. This certificate must never be lightly issued as it is legally binding and can have serious consequences should the failure to comply to the design result in an incident after the issuing of this certificate.

Again ergonomic issues are being addressed and the designer must take into account all ergonomic hazards and attempt to address these hazards by way of alternate designs.

The contractor is required to ensure that all drawings pertaining to the design are kept on site and are available on request by an inspector, contractors, client, client's agent or employee.

What appears to be an unrealistic duty is being placed on the owners of structures to have inspections carried out on new structures six monthly for the first two years and then yearly thereafter. A competent person must carry out this inspection and records of such inspection must be kept. This can be a costly exercise, but that is not the issue, the question that must be asked is what will be identified after two years and also how many structures have actually collapsed after standing for two years or more without any work being carried out on them. The inspection that is required monthly for the first two years may serve a purpose but the inspections thereafter are questionable.

The other question that must be asked is how this is going to be policed and whether it can be effectively policed.

The owner is also required to ensure that the structure after its construction is so maintained to ensure that it remains safe and maintenance records must be kept and be available for inspection by an inspector at all times.

LCA Questions

1. Has the contractor ensured that all reasonable steps have been taken to prevent an uncontrolled collapse of any new or existing structures or part thereof?
2. Has the contractor ensured that no structure is so overloaded that it may become unsafe?
3. Has the designer before a contract goes out for contract ensured that the client has been given all the relevant information on the structure that may affect the pricing of the construction work?
4. Has the designer informed the contractor in writing of any known or anticipated hazards relating to the construction work?
5. Has the designer ensured that the following information is included in a report given to the contractor:
   - geo-science technical report where applicable;
   - the loading the structure is designed to withstand; and
   - the methods and sequence of construction process?
6. Has the designer ensured that the use of dangerous procedures or materials hazardous to the health and safety of persons is avoided by modifying the design or substituting materials?
7. Has the designer taking into consideration subsequent maintenance in the design process in order to minimise the risk?
8. Does the designer carry out regular inspections on site to ensure compliance to the design?
9. Has a record of the designer's inspections been kept?
10. Has the designer stopped the contractor from working should he or she detect that compliance with the design is not being maintained?
11. Has the designer carried out a final inspection and issued a completion certificate to the contractor?
12. Has the designer taken into consideration ergonomics during the life cycle of the construction?
13. Have all the contractors ensured that all drawings are kept on site and are available for inspection by an inspector, contractors, client, client's agent or employee?
14. Has the owner of all structures that are less than two years old ensured that a competent person has carried out inspection on the safety of the structure every six months?
15. Has the owner of all structures that are more than two years old ensured that a competent person has carried out inspection on the safety of the structure every year?
16. Are the records of these inspections available for inspection of an inspector on request?
17. Has the owner of a structure ensured that such structure is maintained in a safe condition?
18. Has the owner of a structure ensured that maintenance records are being kept?

Regulation 10: Formwork and support work

A contractor shall ensure that—

(a) all formwork and support work operations are carried out under the supervision of a competent person who has been appointed in writing for that purpose;

(b) all formwork and support work structures are adequately designed, erected, supported, braced and maintained so that they will be capable of supporting all anticipated vertical and lateral loads that may be applied to them and also that no loads are imposed onto the structure that the structure is not designed to withstand;

(c) the designs of formwork and support work structures are done with close reference to the structural design drawings and where any uncertainty exists, the structural designer should be consulted;

(d) all drawings pertaining to the design of formwork or support work structures are kept on the site and are available on request by an inspector, contractor, client, client's agent or employee;

(e) all equipment used in the formwork or support work structure are carefully examined and checked for suitability by a competent person, before being used;

(f) all formwork and support work structures are inspected by a competent person immediately before, during and after the placement of concrete or any other imposed load and thereafter on a daily basis until the formwork and support work structure has been removed and the results have been recorded in a register and made available on site;

(g) if, after erection, any formwork and support work structure is found to be damaged or weakened to such a degree that its integrity is affected, it shall be safely removed or reinforced immediately;

(h) adequate precautionary measures are taken in order to—

(i) secure any deck panels against displacement; and

(ii) prevent any person from slipping on support work or formwork due to the application of formwork or support work release agents;

(i) as far as is reasonably practicable, the health of any person is not affected through the use of solvents or oils or any other similar substances;

(j) upon casting concrete, the support work or formwork structure should be left in place until the concrete has acquired sufficient strength to support safely, not only its own weight, but also any imposed loads and not removed until authorisation has been given by the competent person contemplated in paragraph (a);

(k) provision is made for safe access by means of secured ladders or staircases for all work to be carried out above the foundation bearing level;

(l) all employees required to erect, move or dismantle formwork and support work structures are provided with adequate training and instruction to perform these operations safely; and

(m) the foundation conditions are suitable to withstand the weight caused by the formwork and support work structure and any imposed loads such that the formwork and support work structure is stable.

This is also a regulation that has been needed for many years as the failure to ensure that formwork and support work is carried out in a safe manner has contributed to some serious incidents in the past.

Firstly, the contractor is required to appoint in writing a competent person to oversee all formwork and support work. The form work and support work must be designed, erected, supported, braced and maintained to carry the loads that will be applied. When the design is being done consideration of the structure design must also be taken into account and if necessary the structural designer should be consulted. The design of the formwork and support work must not be taken lightly and drawing must be kept on sight and be available on request by an inspector, contractor, client, client's agent or employee.

Inspection must be carried out before, during and after the placement of the concrete and thereafter on a daily basis until the structure are removed. Referral is made to a competent person to carry out this inspection without requiring the appointment of such person. The intention of the legislature in this regard must be established as to who this competent person is and in this instance it is logical to assume that the intention was for the person appointed in terms of sub-regulation (a) to carry out these inspections. This would include the examination of all equipment used prior to the erection of the formwork and support work.

If there is any indication that the safety integrity of the formwork and support work has been affected it must be dismantled or strengthened. After concrete has been placed the formwork and support work must remain in place until the concrete has set sufficiently to be able to hold all loads that are placed thereon.

Provision must also be made to ensure safe access to the formwork and support work at all times. Employees who are required to erect remove or dismantle formwork and support work must be competent to do so and must have received adequate training and information.

An important issue that needs to be addressed is the foundation upon which formwork and support work is erected. It must be established that such foundation will be able to carry the relevant loading.

LCA Questions

1. Has the contractor ensured that all formwork and support work operations are carried out under the supervision competent person appointed in writing?
2. Has the contractor ensured that all formwork and support work structures are adequately designed, erected, supported, braced and maintained so that they will be able to support all anticipated loads?
3. Are all drawings pertaining to formwork and support work kept on site and are available for inspection by an inspector, contractor, client, client's agent or employee?
4. Has the contractor ensured that all framework and support work structures are inspected and checked for suitability by a competent person before being used?
5. Has the contractor ensured that all framework and support work structures are inspected by a competent person before, during and after placement of concrete or any other imposed load and thereafter on a daily basis until the structure is removed?
6. Has a record of these inspections been kept?
7. Has the contractor ensured that should weakened formwork or support structure be detected that they are immediately reinforced?

8. Has the contractor ensured that adequate steps are taken to:
   - secure deck panels against displacement; and
   - prevent any person from slipping on support work?
9. Has the contractor ensured that persons will not be affected by the use of solvents or any oils or other similar substances?
10. Has the contractor upon pouring concrete that it gains sufficient strength before the support work is removed?
11. Has the contractor ensured that safe access has been provided for all support work?
12. Have all employees involved in support work been adequately trained and instructed to perform this work in a safe manner?
13. Are the foundations of the form work adequate to sustain the load that is applied?

Regulation 11: Excavation work

(1) A contractor shall ensure that all excavation work is carried out under the supervision of a competent person who has been appointed in writing.

(2) A contractor shall evaluate, as far as is reasonably practicable, the stability of the ground before excavation work begins.

(3) Every contractor who performs excavation work shall—

(a) take suitable and sufficient steps in order to prevent, as far as is reasonably practicable, any person from being buried or trapped by a fall or dislodgement of material in an excavation;

(b) not require or permit any person to work in an excavation which has not been adequately shored or braced: Provided that shoring and bracing may not be necessary where—

(i) the sides of the excavation are sloped to at least the maximum angle of repose measured relative to the horizontal plane; or

(ii) such an excavation is in stable material: Provided that—

(a) permission being given in writing by the appointed competent person contemplated in subregulation (1) upon evaluation by him or her of the site conditions; and

(b) where any uncertainty pertaining to the stability of the soil still exists, the decision from a professional engineer or a professional technologist competent in excavations shall be decisive and such a decision shall be noted in writing and signed by both the competent person contemplated in subregulation (1) and the professional engineer or technologist, as the case may be;

(c) take steps to ensure that the shoring or bracing contemplated in paragraph (b) is designed and constructed in such a manner rendering it strong enough to support the sides of the excavation in question;

(d) ensure that no load, material, plant or equipment is placed or moved near the edge of any excavation where it is likely to cause its collapse and thereby endangering the

safety of, any person, unless precautions such as the provision of sufficient and suitable shoring or bracing are taken to prevent the sides from collapsing;

(e) ensure that where the stability of an adjoining building, structure or road is likely to be affected by the making of an excavation, the steps are taken that may be necessary to ensure the stability of such building, structure or road and the safety of persons;

(f) cause convenient and safe means of access to be provided to every excavation in which persons are required to work and such access shall not be further than 6m from the point where any worker within the excavation is working;

(g) ascertain as far as is reasonably practicable the location and nature of electricity, water, gas or other similar services which may in any way be affected by the work to be performed, and shall before the commencement of excavation work that may affect any such service, take the steps that may be necessary to render the circumstances safe for all persons involved;

(h) cause every excavation, including all bracing and shoring, to be inspected—

(i) daily, prior to each shift;

(ii) after every blasting operation;

(iii) after an unexpected fall of ground;

(iv) after substantial damage to supports; and

(v) after rain,

by the competent person contemplated in subregulation (1), in order to pronounce the safety of the excavation to ensure the safety of persons, and those results are to be recorded in a register kept on site and made available to an inspector, client, client's agent, contractor or employee upon request;

(i) cause every excavation which is accessible to the public or which is adjacent to public roads or thoroughfares, or whereby the safety of persons may be endangered, to be—

(i) adequately protected by a barrier or fence of at least one metre in height and as close to the excavation as is practicable; and

(ii) provided with warning illuminants or any other clearly visible boundary indicators at night or when visibility is poor;

(j) ensure that all precautionary measures as stipulated for confined spaces as determined in the General Safety Regulations promulgated by Government Notice No. R.1031 of 30 May 1986, as amended, are complied with when entering any excavation;

(k) ensure that, where the excavation work involves the use of explosives, a method statement is developed in accordance with the applicable explosives legislation, by an appointed person who is competent in the use of explosives for excavation work and that the procedures therein are followed; and

(l) cause warning signs to be positioned next to an excavation within which persons are working or carrying out inspections or tests.

One must note that this is an extremely important regulation, particularly when one takes into consideration the large number of incidents relating to this regulation that occur annually which result in the deaths of the persons involved. The building industry is amongst the top three for the most incidents each year, of which cave-ins and collapses form a large portion.

Again a competent person must be appointed in writing to supervise all excavation work that is carried out. A problem that existed in terms of the old General Safety Regulation still exists in terms of these regulations and that is the stability of the ground in which the excavation is to be carried out. This regulation requires the contractor to evaluate the ground in terms of its stability before any excavation work is carried out. The problem that exist is that shoring only needs to be applied if the banks have not been accordingly cut back and the appointed competent person has in writing given permission not to make use of shoring and bracing.

This is a decision that one must give careful thought as it can have serious legal consequences should an incident occur. The old excuse of "I never thought it would collapse" will no longer be acceptable after the horse has bolted. It is recommended that any person appointed to make this decision, in particular where there is any doubt on the stability of the ground, falls back onto the legislation and requires a decision from a professional engineer or professional technologist with the necessary expertise of excavation work, in respect to whether shoring and bracing is necessary. However, whoever makes this decision must realise the seriousness thereof. Remember that the contractor must as far as is reasonably practicable ensure that suitable and sufficient steps are taken to avoid a collapse.

All excavations deeper than 1 m (although it does not state this in the regulation one needs to look at the regulation on the notification of construction work) must be inspected at least daily, after blasting, after an unexpected collapse, damage to any supports and after rain, by the appointed person competent to pronounce an opinion on such excavation. Note that the important issue here is that such person's competence will have to be proven, which is not always easy. Therefore, care must be taken to ensure before making this appointment that such person is in fact competent. These inspections must be entered into a register, which must be kept on site and be made available to an inspector, client, client's agent, contractor or employee.

The following aspects must also be taken into consideration when an excavation is being carried out:

- stability of adjoining buildings, structures or roads;
- the banks of the excavation must not be overloaded;
- safety of persons;
- location and nature of water, gas or other similar services;
- safe access every 12 meters in an excavation of 1 meter deep (a person carrying out work must never be more than 6 meters from an access point).

The following must also be carried out where an excavation is accessible by the public:

- it must be adequately protected by a barrier of fencing at least one meter high and as close to the excavation as is practicable;
- it must be provided with red warning lights or any other clearly visible boundary indicators at night or when visibility conditions are poor.

Again in these regulations the legislature has not deemed it necessary to make reference to danger tape and therefore it must be assumed that danger tape in not acceptable as a barrier for any excavation work.

Where explosives are used then the relevant Explosives Regulations must be adhered to.

Warning signage must be posted where an excavation is being carried out within which persons are working or carrying out inspections.

LCA Questions

1. Has the contractor ensured that all excavation work is carried out under the supervision of a person that is competent and has been appointed in writing?
2. Has the contractor as far as is reasonably practicable evaluated the stability of the ground before excavation work begins?
3. Has the contractor ensured that suitable and sufficient steps are taken to prevent persons from being trapped due to a collapse?
4. Has the contractor ensured that any person working in an excavation which has not been cut back to at least the maximum angle of repose measured relative to the horizontal and where the ground is unstable, without shoring being in place?
5. Has the contractor ensured that the shoring is so designed and constructed to be strong enough to support the sides of the excavation?
6. Has the contractor ensured that the sides of the excavation are not overloaded?
7. Has the contractor ensured that adjacent structures and building are supported if they can be affect by the excavation?
8. Has the contractor ensured that there is a safe and convenient access to the excavation no more than 6 meters from any worker?
9. Has the contractor ensured that all locations of gas, electricity, water and similar services have been established prior to the excavation work being carried out?
10. Has the contractor ensured that all bracing and shoring is inspected:
    - daily, prior to commencement of each shift;
    - after every blasting operation;
    - after an unexpected fall of ground;
    - after substantial damage to supports; and
    - after rain?
11. Does the contractor ensure that when any excavation is made and it is accessible to the public or is adjacent to public roads or thoroughfares or by which persons can be endangered, it is adequately fenced at least 1m high as close to the excavation as practicable?
12. Does the contractor ensure that when any excavation has been done and it is accessible to the public or is adjacent to public roads or thoroughfares or by which persons can be endangered, illuminants or any other clearly visible boundary indicators are provided at night and where the visibility is poor?
13. Does the contractor ensure that the precautionary measures required in terms of confined spaces are met?
14. Does the contractor ensure that when explosives are required to carry out an excavation, that the explosives regulations are adhered to?
15. Does the contractor ensure that warning signs are posted next to an excavation in which persons are working or carrying out inspections or tests?

Regulation 12: Demolition work

(1) A contractor shall appoint a competent person in writing to supervise and control all demolition work on site.

(2) A contractor shall ensure that prior to any demolition work being carried out, and in order also to ascertain the method of demolition to be used, a detailed structural engineering survey of the structure to be demolished is carried out by a competent person and that a method statement on the procedure to be followed in demolishing the structure is developed.

(3) During the demolition, a competent person shall check the structural integrity of the structure at intervals determined in the method statement contemplated in subregulation (2), in order to avoid any premature collapses.

(4) Every contractor who performs demolition work shall—

(a) with regard to a structure being demolished, take steps to ensure that—

(i) no floor, roof or other part of the structure is overloaded with debris or material in a manner which would render it unsafe;

(ii) all reasonably practicable precautions are taken to avoid the danger of the structure collapsing when any part of the framing of a framed or partly framed building is removed, or when reinforced concrete is cut; and

(iii) precautions are taken in the form of adequate shoring or such other means as may be necessary to prevent the accidental collapse of any part of the structure or adjoining structure;

(b) not require or permit any person to work under overhanging material or structure, which has not been adequately supported, shored or braced;

(c) take steps to ensure that any support, shoring or bracing contemplated in paragraph (b), is designed and constructed so that it is strong enough to support the overhanging material;

(d) where the stability of an adjoining building, structure or road is likely to be affected by demolition work on a structure, take such steps as may be necessary to ensure the stability of such structure or road and the safety of persons;

(e) ascertain as far as is reasonably practicable the location and nature of electricity, water, gas or other similar services which may in anyway, be affected by the work to be performed, and shall before the commencement of demolition work that may affect any such service, take the steps that may be necessary to render circumstances safe for all persons involved;

(f) cause every stairwell used and every floor where work is being performed in a building being demolished, to be adequately illuminated by either natural or artificial means;

(g) cause convenient and safe means of access to be provided to every part of the demolition site in which persons are required to work; and

(h) erect a catch platform or net above an entrance or passageway or above a place where persons work or pass under, or fence off the danger area if work is being performed above such entrance, passageway, or place so as to ensure that all persons are kept safe where there is a danger or possibility of persons being struck by falling objects.

(5) A contractor shall ensure that no material is dropped to any point, which falls outside the exterior walls of the structure, unless the area is effectively protected.

(6) Waste and debris shall not be disposed from a high place by a chute unless the chute—

(a) is adequately constructed and rigidly fastened;

(b) if inclined at an angle of more than 45 degrees to the horizontal, is enclosed on its four sides;

(c) if of the open type, is inclined at an angle of less than 45 degrees to the horizontal;

(d) where necessary, is fitted with a gate at the bottom end to control the flow of material; and

(e) is discharged into a container or an enclosed area surrounded by barriers.

(7) A contractor shall ensure that every chute used to dispose of rubble is designed in such a manner that rubble does not free-fall and that the chute is strong enough to withstand the force of the debris traveling along the chute.

(8) A contractor shall ensure that equipment is not used on floors or working surfaces, unless such floors or surfaces are of sufficient strength to support the imposed loads.

(9) Where the risk assessment indicates the presence of asbestos, a contractor shall ensure that all asbestos related work is conducted in accordance with the provisions of the Asbestos Regulations promulgated by Government Notice No. R.155 of 10 February 2002, as amended.

(10) Where the risk assessment indicates the presence of lead, a contractor shall ensure that all lead related work is conducted in accordance with the provisions of the Lead Regulations promulgated by Government Notice No. R.236 of 28 February 2002, as amended.

(11) Where the demolition work involves the use of explosives, a method statement is to be developed in accordance with the applicable explosives legislation, by an appointed person who is competent in the use of explosives for demolition work and the procedures therein are adhered to.

(12) A contractor shall ensure that all waste and debris is as soon as reasonably practicable removed and disposed of from the site in accordance with the applicable legislation.

Again a competent person must be appointed in writing to supervise all excavation work that is carried out. The contractor must ensure that a method of demolition is established and a competent person must carry out a detailed structural engineering survey of the structure to be demolished and this must be included into the method of demolition. During the process of demolition a competent person must continuously check the integrity of the structure in order to prevent premature collapse.

Here reference is made to three competent persons and the question is whether it is the same person or not. It can be confusing, however there is no reason why it cannot be the same person as long as such person has the necessary expertise, if not, then there will be three people each having the applicable expertise.

The structure being demolished must at no stage be overloaded and all steps must be taken to prevent an uncontrolled collapse, in particular when reinforcing or frames are being removed. Adequate shoring must be applied and only removed when safe to do so.

The following also needs to be addressed:

- no person may work under overhanging material or structure not adequately supported;
- supports to be strong enough to sustain loads;

- adjoining buildings, structures or roads not to be affected by demolition;
- ascertain location and nature of electricity, water, gar or similar services;
- cause every stairwell or floor where work is to be carried out to be adequately illuminated;
- provide convenient and safe access to every part where persons are required to work;
- erect a catch platform or net where there is a risk of falling objects;
- do not drop material or debris to any point outside the perimeter unless barricaded.

Waste and debris disposed of from a height must be via a chute, which is:

- adequately constructed and rigidly fastened;
- inclined at more than 45 degrees;
- enclosed on all four sides;
- if of open type inclination to be less than 45 degrees;
- be fitted with a gate to control material at the bottom;
- discharged into a container or enclosed area;
- rubble is not to freefall;
- all rubble must be disposed of as soon as possible.

Where the risk assessments indicate the presence of either asbestos or lead, the relevant Asbestos and Lead Regulations must be adhered to. Where explosives are used, then the relevant Explosives Regulations must be adhered to.

LCA Questions

1. Has the contractor ensured that all demolition work is carried out under the supervision of a person that is competent and has been appointed in writing?
2. Has the contractor ensured that a detailed structural engineering survey of the structure to be demolished, has been carried out by a competent person?
3. Has the contractor ensured that a method statement on the procedure to be followed on the demolition of a structure has been developed?
4. Has the contractor ensured that during the demolition process that a competent person carries out inspections of the structure as required in terms of the method statement and to ensure that the structure does not prematurely collapse?
5. Does the contractor ensure that when any structure is being demolished, all roofs, floors or other parts are not overloaded with debris?
6. Does the contractor ensure that when any structure is being demolished, all practical precautions are taken to prevent the collapse of the structure when any part of the frame is removed (framed buildings)?
7. Does the contractor ensure that when any structure is being demolished, adequate shoring is in place to prevent any collapse?
8. Does the contractor ensure that when any structure is being demolished, no person works under unsupported overhangs that have not been adequately shored?

9. Does the contractor ensure that when any structure is being demolished, adequate shoring is in place to prevent an adjoining building from collapsing?
10. Does the employer ensure that when any structure is being demolished, all shoring is designed and constructed to be strong enough?
11. Does the contractor ensure that when any structure is being demolished, the location and nature of electricity, water, gas or similar services are established and that steps are taken to render persons safe?
12. Does the contractor ensure that every stairwell used and every floor where work is being performed is adequately illuminated?
13. Does the contractor ensure that safe means of access is provided to every part of the building site?
14. Has the contractor ensured that a catch net or platform has been erected to protect persons from being injured by falling objects?
15. Has the contractor ensured that no material is dropped to any point that falls outside the exterior walls unless the area is effectively proceed?
16. Has the contractor ensured that when waste and debris is disposed of from a height through a chute that the chute:
    - is adequately constructed and rigidly fastened;
    - if inclined at an angle of more than 45 degrees to the horizontal, is enclosed on its four sides;
    - is fitted with a gate at the bottom to control flow; and
    - is discharged into a container or an enclosed area surrounded by barriers?
17. Has the contractor ensured that the chute is designed to be strong enough?
18. Has the contractor ensured that all the floors on which work is being carried out on are of adequate strength and are able to sustain their load?
19. Where the risk assessment has indicated the presence of asbestos has the contractor complied with the requirements of the Asbestos Regulations?
20. Where the risk assessment has indicated the presence of lead has the contractor complied with the requirements of the Lead Regulations?
21. Where explosives are use in the demolition process has the contractor ensured that a method statement is in place and that the work is carried out under the supervision of a competent person?
22. Has the contractor ensured that all waste and debris is removed from site as soon as possible?

Regulation 13: Tunneling

(1) Any contractor performing tunneling activities shall comply with the Tunneling Regulations as published under the Mine Health and Safety Act, 1996 (Act No. 29 of 1996), as amended.

(2) Notwithstanding the provisions of subregulation (1), no person shall enter a tunnel, which has a height dimension of less than 800 mm.

Any person carrying out tunneling work is required to adhere to the requirements relating to tunneling in the Mine Health and Safety Act. Over and above this requirements the legislature deemed it necessary to require that no person may enter into a tunnel of less than 800 mm in height.

LCA Questions

1. Does the contractor carrying out tunneling have a copy of the Mine Health and Safety Act on the site?
2. Does the contractor ensure that all tunneling is carried out in terms of the Mine Health and Safety Act?
3. Does the contractor ensure that persons do not enter into a tunnel with a dimension of less than 600 mm?

Regulation 14: Scaffolding

(1) Every contractor using access scaffolding, shall ensure that such scaffolding, when used, complies with the safety standards incorporated for this purpose into these Regulations under section 44 of the Act.

(2) A contractor shall ensure that all scaffolding work operations are carried out under the supervision of a competent person who has been appointed in writing and that all scaffold erectors, team leaders and inspectors are competent to carry out their work.

In terms of this regulation a competent person needs to be appointed in writing to supervise scaffolding operations and all erectors, team leaders and inspectors must be competent to carry out their tasks. It is interesting to note that reference is made to an inspector of scaffolding who does not have to be appointed, it would have been logical to require the competent person to do all the tasks that may be envisaged to be carried out by the so called inspector.

All scaffolding has to comply with SABS 085 "The design, erection, use and inspection of access scaffolding". This means that there must be a copy of this code on the site where scaffolding operations are being undertaken.

Although the scaffolding has to comply with this code the old General Safety Regulations will go a long way to achieve this compliance.

LCA Questions

1. Do all contractors that make use of scaffolding have on site a copy of SABS 085 as amended?
2. Do all contractors ensure that all scaffolding is in compliance to SABS 085?
3. Has the contractor carrying out scaffolding work appointed a competent person in writing to supervise all scaffolding operations?
4. Has the contractor ensured that all scaffold erectors, team leaders and inspectors are competent to carry out their work?

Regulation 15: Suspended platforms

(1) A contractor shall ensure that all suspended platform work operations are carried out under the supervision of a competent person who has been appointed in writing, and that all suspended platform erectors, operators and inspectors are competent to carry out their work.

(2) No contractor shall use or permit the use of a suspended platform, unless—

(a) the design, stability and construction thereof comply with the safety standards incorporated for this purpose into these Regulations under section 44 of the Act;

(b) he or she is in possession of a certificate of system design issued by a professional engineer, certificated engineer or a professional technologist for the use of the suspended platform system; and

(c) he or she is, prior to the commencement of the work, in possession of an operational compliance plan developed by a competent person based on the certificate of system design contemplated in paragraph (b) and applicable to the environment in which the system is being used, this must include proof of the—

(i) competent person who has been appointed for supervision;

(ii) competency of erectors, operators and inspectors;

(iii) operational design calculations which should comply with the requirements of the system design certificate;

(iv) performance test results;

(v) sketches indicating the completed system with the operational loading capacity of the platform;

(vi) procedures for and records of inspections having been carried out; and

(vii) procedures for and records of maintenance work having been carried out:

Provided that subregulation (2) shall only become applicable six months from the date of promulgation of these regulations.

(3) A contractor making use of a suspended platform system shall forward a copy of the certificate of system design issued by a professional engineer, certificated engineer or professional technologist including a copy of the design calculations, sketches and test results, to the provincial director before commencement of the use of the system and must further indicate the intended type of work the system would be used for.

(4) A contractor need not re-submit a copy of the certificate of system design contemplated in subregulation (3) for every new project: Provided that the environment in which the system is being used does not change to such an extent that the system design certificate is no longer applicable and, should uncertainty exist of the applicability of the system design certificate, the decision of a professional engineer, certificated engineer or professional technologist shall be decisive.

(5) A contractor shall ensure that the outriggers of each suspended platform—

(a) are constructed of steel or any other material of similar strength and have a safety factor of at least four in relation to the load it is to carry; and

(b) have suspension points provided with stop devices or other effective devices at the outer ends to prevent the displacement of ropes.

(6) A contractor shall ensure that—

(a) the parts of the building or structure on which the outriggers are supported, are checked by means of calculations to ensure that the required safety factor is adhered to without risk of damage to the building or structure;

(b) the suspension wire rope and the safety wire rope are separately connected to the outrigger;

(c) each person on a suspended platform is provided with and wears a safety harness as a fall prevention device which must at all times, be attached to the suspended

platform or to the anchorage points on the structure whilst on the suspended platform;

(d) *the hand or power driven machinery to be used for the lifting or lowering of the working platform of a suspended platform is constructed and maintained in such a manner that an uncontrolled movement of the working platform cannot occur;*

(e) *the machinery referred to in paragraph (d) is so situated that it is easily accessible for inspection;*

(f) *the rope connections to the outriggers are vertically above the connections to the working platform; and*

(g) *where the working platform is suspended by two ropes only, the connections of the ropes to the working platform are of such height above the level of the working platform as to ensure the stability of the working platform.*

(7) A contractor shall ensure that the suspended platform—

(a) *is suspended as near as possible to the structure to which work is being done and, except when light work is being done, is secured at every working position to prevent horizontal movement between the suspended platform and the structure;*

(b) *is fitted with anchorage points to which workers shall attach the lanyard of the safety harness worn and used by the worker and such anchorage connections shall have sufficient strength to withstand any potential load applied to it; and*

(c) *is fitted with a conspicuous notice easily understandable by all workers working with the suspended platform, showing the maximum mass load which the suspended platform can carry.*

(8) A contractor shall cause—

(a) *the whole installation and all working parts of the suspended platform to be thoroughly examined in accordance with the manufacturer's specification;*

(b) *the whole installation to be subjected to a performance test as determined by the standard to which the suspended platform was manufactured;*

(c) *the performance test contemplated in paragraph (b) to be done by a competent person appointed in writing with the knowledge and experience of erection and maintenance of suspended platforms or similar machinery and who shall determine the serviceability of the structures, ropes, machinery and safety devices before they are used, every time suspended platforms are erected;*

(d) *the performance test contemplated in paragraph (b) of the whole installation of the suspended platform to be subjected to a load equal to that prescribed by the manufacturer or, in the absence of such load, to a load of 110 per cent of the rated mass load, at intervals not exceeding 12 months and in such a manner that every part of the installation is stressed accordingly.*

(9) Notwithstanding the provisions of subregulation (8), the contractor shall cause every hoisting rope, hook or other load-attaching device which forms part of the suspended platform to be thoroughly examined in accordance with the manufacturer's specification by the competent person contemplated in subregulation (8) before they are used following every time they are assembled, and, in cases of continuous use, at intervals not exceeding three months.

(10) A contractor shall ensure that the suspended platform supervisor appointed in terms of the provisions of subregulation (1), or the suspended platform inspector mentioned in subregulation (1), carries out a daily inspection of all the equipment prior to use, including establishing whether—

(a) all connection bolts are secure;

(b) all safety devices are functioning;

(c) all safety devices are not tampered with or vandalized;

(d) the maximum mass load of the platform is not exceeded;

(e) the occupants in the suspended platform are using safety harnesses which have been properly attached;

(f) there are no visible signs of damage to the equipment; and

(g) all reported operating problems have been attended to.

(11) A contractor shall ensure that all inspection and performance test records are kept on the construction site at all times and made available to an inspector, client, client's agent or employee upon request.

(12) A contractor shall ensure that all employees required to work or to be supported on a suspended platform are—

(a) physically and psychologically fit to work safely in such an environment by being in possession of a medical certificate of fitness;

(b) competent in conducting work related to suspended platforms safely;

(c) trained or had received training which include at least—

(i) how to access and egress the suspended platform safely;

(ii) how to correctly operate the controls and safety devices of the equipment;

(iii) information on the dangers related to the misuse of safety devices; and

(iv) information on the procedures to be followed in the case of—

(aa) an emergency;

(bb) the malfunctioning of equipment;

(cc) the discovery of a suspected defect in the equipment; and

(v) instructions on the proper use of safety harnesses.

(13) Where the outrigger is to be moved, the contractor shall ensure that only persons trained and competent to effect such move, perform this task and that an inspection be carried out and the results thereof be recorded by the competent person prior to re-use of the suspended platform.

(14) A contractor shall ensure that the suspended platform is properly isolated after use at the end of each working day such that no part of the suspended platform will present a danger to any person thereafter.

Although SABS EN 1808 "Safety requirements on suspended Access equipment – Design calculations, stability criteria, construction tests', has been incorporated the legislature has deemed it necessary to add further requirements due to mainly the amount of accidents that have occurred involving this equipment.

A competent person has to be appointed in writing to supervise the use of this equipment.

This equipment has to be designed by a professional engineer, certificated engineer or a professional technologist and the contractor making use of such equipment must be in possession of a certificate of design. The competent person has to develop a compliance plan based on the certificate of design prior to the use of this equipment and must include at least the following:

- Competent person details;
- Details of competency of erectors, operators and inspectors;
- That operational design calculations comply with the system design specifications;
- The performance test results;
- Sketches;
- The procedure and records of inspections; and
- The procedure and record of all maintenance.

A copy of the system design is to be forwarded to the regional director. This does not have to be forwarded for every new project if there has been no change to the design.

The rest of this regulation is largely self explanatory and needs to be read and studied in detail.

LCA Questions

1. Has every contractor ensured that all suspended scaffolding complies with SABS EN 1808 or SABS 1903?
2. Has every contractor appointed in writing a competent person to supervise suspended scaffold work?
3. Has every contractor ensured that when suspended scaffold work is carried out that all erectors, operators and inspectors are competent to carry out their work?
4. Are all contractor making use of suspended scaffold in possession of a certificate of system design issued by a professional engineer, certificated engineer or a professional technologist for the use of the suspended scaffold?
5. Have all the contractors making use of suspended scaffolding, prior to commencement of work, ensured that they are in possession of an operational compliance plan developed by a competent person, which is based on the certificate of system design?
6. Does the operational compliance plan include the following:
   - proof of the competent person appointed;
   - proof of competency of erectors, operators and inspectors;
   - proof of the operational design calculations
   - proof of the performance results;
   - proof of sketches indicating the completed system for operational loading capacity of the platform;
   - proof of the procedures for the records of inspections having been carried out? and
   - proof of the procedures for and records of maintenance work having been carried out?

7. Has the contractor making use of a suspended scaffold forwarded to the provincial director a copy of the certificate of system design, together with a copy of the design calculations, sketches and test results and for what purpose the scaffold is to be used?
8. Have all contractors making use of a suspended scaffold made sure that the outriggers:
   - are constructed of steel or material of similar strength with a factor of safety of at least 4; and
   - that the suspension points are so designed with effective stop devices to prevent the displacement of ropes?
9. Have all contractors making use of a suspended scaffold made sure that:
   - the safety factor of the structure is such that it can carry the load;
   - suspension rope and the safety rope are separately connected to the outrigger;
   - each person on the scaffold wears a safety harness attached at all times to the
   - platform or the structure;
   - the hand or power driven machinery used for raising or lowering of the suspended scaffold is so designed and maintained to prevent the uncontrolled movement of the platform;
   - is the lifting equipment so installed for easy inspection;
   - the ropes are connected vertically above the working platform; and
   - when there are only two connecting ropes that they are so fitted to ensure that stability of the platform?
10. Has the contractor ensured that the suspended platform:
    - is as close to the structure as possible;
    - is secured in position except when light work is performed;
    - is fitted with anchorage points for safety harnesses; and
    - is fitted with a sign easily understandable indicating the maximum mass load?
11. Have all the contractors making use of suspended scaffolds:
    - had the entire installation inspected according to the manufacturer's specifications;
    - caused them to be load tested; and
    - caused them to be tested by a competent person?
12. Have all the hoisting ropes and attaching devices been inspected on assembly and then at least once every three months?
13. Has the contractor ensured that the suspended scaffold is inspected by the competent person or the inspector daily prior to being made use of?
14. Does the inspection ensure the following:
    - all connection bolts are secure;
    - all safety devices are functioning;
    - all safety devices have not been tampered with or vandalised;
    - the maximum mass load of the platform is not exceeded;

- that the occupants make use of safety harnesses;
- that there are no visible signs of damage to the equipment; and
- that all reported operating problems have been addressed?

15. Has the contractor ensured that all records of tests and inspections are available for inspection?
16. Has the contractor ensured that all employees working on or with a suspended scaffold are:
    - physically and psychologically fit for this environment and are in possession of a medically certificate of fitness;
    - competent to perform the work; and
    - are trained?
17. Have the workers been trained on the following:
    - how to access and egress the platform safely;
    - how to correctly operate;
    - the hazards of the job;
    - the procedures to follow in the case of an emergency, the malfunctioning of the equipment and the detection of a suspected defect; and
    - the proper use of the safety harnesses?
18. Has the contractor ensured that the moving of the suspended scaffold is done by trained and competent persons under the supervision of the appointed competent person?
19. Have the results of the moving been recorded?
20. Has the contractor ensured that after use that the suspended scaffold is so isolated that persons will be placed in any form of danger?

Regulation 16: Boatswains chairs

(1) A contractor shall ensure that every boatswain's chair or similar device is securely suspended and is constructed in such a manner so as to prevent any occupant from falling therefrom.

(2) The contractor shall ensure that an inspection is carried out prior and a performance test immediately after, the boatswain chair has been erected and thereafter a visual inspection should be carried out on a daily basis prior to use.

This regulation is self-explanatory and it is important that it be read. It is interesting to note that this form of scaffolding is seldom used other than on ships. A new aspect that has been included into this regulation is the fact that the boatswain chair must be inspected and tested. An inspection prior to use and a load test immediately after erection and then an inspection must be carried out daily thereafter.

It is questionable as to what is going to be gained in terms of the load test and also how the legislature envisaged this must be done.

LCA Questions

1. Has the contractor ensured that every boatswain chair is securely suspended?
2. Has the contractor ensured that the boatswain's chair is so constructed as to prevent a person from falling out?
3. Has the contractor ensured that an inspection is carried out prior and a performance test immediately after, the boatswain chair has been erected?
4. Has the contractor ensured that all boatswains chairs are inspected on a daily basis prior to use?

Regulation 17: Material hoist

(1) A contractor shall ensure that every material hoist and its tower have been constructed of sound material in accordance with the generally accepted technical standards and are strong enough and free from defects.

(2) A contractor shall cause the tower of every material hoist to be—

(a) erected on firm foundations and secured to the structure or braced by steel wire guy ropes and to extend to such a distance above the highest landing as to allow a clear and unobstructed space of at least 900 mm for overtravel;

(b) enclosed on all sides at the bottom, and at all floors where persons are at risk of being struck by moving parts of the hoist, except on the side or sides giving access to the material hoist, with walls or other effective means to a height of at least 2 100 mm from the ground or floor level; and

(c) provided with a door or gate at least 2 100 mm in height at each landing and such door or gate shall be kept closed, except when the platform is at rest at such a landing.

(3) A contractor shall cause—

(a) the platform of every material hoist to be designed in such a manner that it shall safely contain the loads being conveyed and that the combined weight of the platform and the load does not exceed the designed lifting capacity of the hoist;

(b) the hoisting rope of every material hoist which has a remote winch to be effectively protected from damage by any external cause to the portion of the hoisting rope between the winch and the tower of the hoist; and

(c) every material hoist to be provided with an efficient brake capable of holding the platform with its maximum load in any position when the power is not being supplied to the hoisting machinery.

(4) No contractor shall require or permit trucks, barrows or material to be conveyed on the platform of a material hoist and no person shall so convey trucks, barrows or material unless such articles are so secured or contained in such a manner that displacement thereof cannot take place during movement.

(5) A contractor shall cause a notice, indicating the maximum mass load which may be carried at any one time and the prohibition of persons from riding on the platform of the material hoist, to be affixed around the base of the tower and at each landing.

(6) A contractor of a material hoist shall not require or permit any person to operate such a hoist, unless the person is competent in the operation thereof.

(7) No contractor shall require or permit any person to ride on a material hoist.

(8) A contractor shall cause every material hoist—

(a) to be inspected on a daily basis by a competent person who has been appointed in writing and has the experience pertaining to the erection and maintenance of material hoists or similar machinery;

(b) inspection contemplated in paragraph (a), to include the determination of the serviceability of the entire material hoist including guides, ropes and their connections, drums, sheaves or pulleys and all safety devices;

(c) inspection results to be entered and signed in a record book, which shall be kept on the premises for that purpose;

(d) to be properly maintained and that the maintenance records in this regard are kept on site.

This regulation has basically been transferred from the Driven Machinery Regulations where is was known as "builders hoist".

The requirements of this regulation are similar to those in the case of a goods hoist found in the Driven Machinery Regulations, except that there are issues that relate specifically to a material hoist. These hoists do not normally run within a hatchway and are normally of a cantilever type.

The tower of such a hoist is required to be constructed of sound material, to be strong enough and free from patent defects and in general to be constructed according to generally accepted technical standards. The user is required to cause every tower of every material hoist:

- to be secured to the structure or to be braced by steel-wire guy ropes and to extend to such a distance above the highest landing as to allow a clear and unobstructed space of at least 900 mm for over-travel
- to be enclosed on all sides, at the bottom and at all floors where persons are liable to be struck by moving parts of the hoist, except on the side or sides giving access to the conveyance, with walls or other effective means to a height of at least 2 100 mm from the ground or floor level
- to be provided with a door or gate at least 2 100 mm high at each landing, and such door or gate shall be kept closed, except when the conveyance is at such landing.

Note that there is no requirement for mechanical or electrical type locks, since these are portable machines, which are run by independent petrol-driven engines in most instances, and it is also impractical. Although these requirements in the building industry are very seldom complied with and many notices are served in this regard, very few incidents involving such machinery are reported.

Sub-regulation (3) deals with the requirements relating to the conveyance itself, including the operation thereof. It is the user's duty to ensure that:

- the conveyance is to be designed to safely carry any load it may be required to carry;
- in the case where there is a remote hoist the ropes must be adequately protected against any damage by any external source;
- every builders' hoist is provided with an efficient brake capable of holding the maximum mass load in any position when the power is not being supplied to the hoisting machinery.

It is interesting to note that the previous requirement of a signalling system to be in place has not been included into these regulations and no replacement system has been included.

Sub-regulation (4) requires that all equipment and material that is conveyed on such a hoist is so secured or contained that it cannot be displaced. What is interesting in this sub-regulation is that the legislature deemed it necessary to place a duty on both the user and any other person that would be involved in the operation of such machine, which means that both the user and the person involved in the operation of such machine can be prosecuted for the same offence. The same applies with respect to the prohibition of persons to ride on a hoist, in that the duty rests with both the user and any person not to do so.

A new aspect that persons from riding thereon has been included is that the contractor is required to cause a notice to be posted at the base and at each landing indicating the maximum mass load and also profiting persons from riding thereon. The contractor shall also not allow any person to ride on such a hoist. This places a duty on the contractor to manage this aspect.

The legislature also clearly states that the operator of such a hoist must be competent to operate it.

Finally, sub-regulation (8) requires that every builders' hoist be inspected daily by a person who competent and has been appointed in writing. The inspection must include an inspection of the serviceability of the entire hoist including guides, ropes and their connections, drums, sheaves or pulleys and all safety devices. The results of the inspection must be entered into a record book, to be kept on the premises. The material hoist must be properly maintained and maintenance records to be kept on site.

LCA Questions

1. Are all builders hoist towers constructed in accordance with an acceptable standard?
2. Does every builders hoist tower have a clear and unobstructed space of 900 mm for over travel?
3. Is every builders hoist tower enclosed on all sides at the bottom?
4. Is every builders hoist tower enclosed on landings where moving parts may be accessible?
5. Is every builders hoist tower enclosed to a height of at least 2 100 mm?
6. Is every builders hoist tower provided with a gate on each landing?
7. Is every builders hoist tower landing gate at least 1 800 mm high?
8. Is every builders hoist tower gate kept closed at all times whilst the conveyance is not on that landing?
9. Is the builders hoist supplied with an efficient braking system which will hold the hoist in position when the power is off?
10. Are articles that are carried in the conveyance so held that they cannot be displaced whilst the hoist is in motion?
11. Are persons prohibited from riding in the hoist?
12. Has a notice been posted indicating the maximum mass load and prohibiting persons from travelling therein?
13. Have the notices been posted at the bottom and at every landing?
14. Are all material hoists inspected daily by an appointed competent person?
15. Are the inspection results entered into a record?
16. Are material hoists properly maintained and records thereof kept?

Regulation 18: Batch plants

(1) A contractor shall ensure that all batch plants are operated and supervised by a competent person who has been appointed in writing.

(2) A contractor shall ensure that the placement and erection of a batch plant complies with the requirements set out by the manufacturer and that such plant is erected as designed.

(3) A contractor shall ensure that all devices to start and stop a batch plant are provided and that these devices are—

(a) placed in an easily accessible position; and

(b) constructed in such a manner as to prevent accidental starting.

(4) The contractor shall ensure that the machinery and plant selected is suitable for the task and that all dangerous moving parts of a mixer are placed beyond the reach of persons by means of doors, covers or other similar means.

(5) No person shall be permitted to remove or modify any guard or safety equipment relating to a batch plant, unless authorized to do so by the appointed person as contemplated in subregulation (1).

(6) A contractor shall ensure that all persons authorized to operate the batch plant are fully—

(a) aware of all the dangers involved in the operation thereof; and

(b) conversant with the precautionary measures to be taken in the interest of health and safety.

(7) No person supervising or operating a batch plant shall authorize any other person to operate the plant, unless such person is competent to operate such machinery.

(8) A contractor shall ensure that all precautionary measures as stipulated for confined spaces in the General Safety Regulations promulgated by Government Notice No. R.1031 dated 30 May 1986, as amended, are adhered to when entering any silo.

(9) A contractor shall ensure that a record is kept of any repairs or maintenance to a batch plant and that it is made available, on site, to an inspector, client, client's agent or employee upon request.

(10) A contractor shall ensure that all lifting machines and lifting tackle used in the operation of a batch plant complies with the requirements of the Driven Machinery Regulations promulgated by Government Notice No. R.295 dated 26 February 1988, as amended.

(11) A contractor shall ensure that all precautionary measures are adhered to regarding the usage of electrical equipment in explosive atmospheres, when entering a silo, as contemplated in the Electrical Installation Regulations promulgated by Government Notice No. R.2271 dated 11 October 1995, as amended.

It is interesting as to why the legislature specifically included "batch plants" as these plants are machinery and are addressed quite adequately by the machinery regulations. Again the legislature deemed it necessary to ensure that a competent person is appointed in writing to manage and supervise the operation of these plants.

This regulation is totally self-explanatory and is in line with the machinery regulations that have already been addressed by the machinery regulations and need no further discussion.

LCA Questions

1. Has the contractor ensured that all batch plants are operated under the supervision of an appointed competent person?
2. Has the contractor ensured that that all batch plants are erected according to the manufacturer's requirements?
3. Has the contractor ensured that there are devices to stop and start the batch plant?
4. Are the stop and start buttons placed in such a position that they are easily and readily accessible and so constructed to prevent accidental starting?
5. Has the contractor ensured that the moving parts of a mixer are beyond the normal reach of any person by way of covers and doors or similar means?
6. Are steps taken to ensure that persons do not interfere and modify any guards without the permission of the appointed competent person?
7. Are all persons who operate batch plants trained and informed of the dangers and conversant with the precautionary measures?
8. Are only competent persons allowed to operate the batch plant?
9. When a silo is being entered has the contractor ensured the General Safety Regulations relating to confined spaces are adhered to?
10. Has the contractor ensured that there is a record of all maintenance of the batch plant and that it is available for inspection by an inspector, client, client's agent or employee?
11. Has the contractor ensured that all lifting machines and tackle used on the batch plant comply with the requirements of the Driven Machinery Regulations?
12. Has the contractor ensured that when entering a silo which may have an explosive atmosphere, that the Explosive Regulations are complied with?

Regulation 19: Explosive powered tools

(1) No contractor shall use or permit any person to use an explosive powered tool, unless—

(a) it is provided with a protective guard around the muzzle end, which effectively confines any flying fragments or particles; and

(b) the firing mechanism is so designed that the explosive powered tool will not function unless—

(i) it is held against the surface with a force of at least twice its weight; and

(ii) the angle of inclination of the barrel to the work surface is not more then 15 degrees from a right angle:

Provided that the provisions of this subregulation shall not apply to explosive powered tools in which the energy of the cartridge is transmitted to the bolts, nails or similar relevant objects by means of an intermediate piston which has a limited distance of travel.

(2) A contractor shall ensure that—

(a) only cartridges suited for the explosive powered tool and the work to be performed are used;

(b) the explosive powered tool is cleaned and examined daily before use and as often as may be necessary for its safe operation by a competent person who has been appointed;

(c) that the safety devices are in proper working order prior to use;

(d) when not in use, the explosive powered tool and the cartridges are locked up in a safe place, which is inaccessible to unauthorised persons;

(e) the explosive powered tool is not stored in a loaded condition;

(f) a warning notice is displayed in a conspicuous manner wherever the explosive powered tool is used;

(g) the issuing and collection of cartridges and nails or studs is—

(i) controlled and done in writing by a person having been appointed in writing; and

(ii) recorded in a register and that the recipient has accordingly signed for the receipt thereof as well as the returning of any spent and unspent cartridges.

(3) No contractor shall permit or require any person to use an explosive powered tool unless such person has been—

(a) provided with and uses suitable protective equipment; and

(b) trained in the operation, maintenance and use of such a tool.

No major changes have been made to this regulation and it has merely been taken out of the Driven Machinery Regulations and placed into these.

An explosive powered tool must be fitted with a protective guard around the muzzle, which will effectively confine any flying fragments or particles. The firing mechanism must be so designed that the tool will not operate unless:

- it is held against the surface with a force of at least twice its weight;
- the angle of inclination of the barrel to the work surface is not more than 15 degrees from the right angle.

These requirements do not apply to explosive powered tools in which the energy of the cartridge is transmitted to the bolts, nails or similar relevant objects by means of an intermediate piston, which has a limited distance of travel – in other words, nothing can be fired from the explosive powered tool and therefore it cannot be used as a firearm.

In terms of sub-regulation (2) the user shall ensure that:

- only cartridges suited to explosive powered tools and the work to be performed are used;
- the tool is cleaned and examined at the regular intervals as may be necessary for its safe operation;
- when not in use, the explosive powered tool and the cartridges are stored in a safe place which is inaccessible to unauthorized persons;
- the explosive powered tool is not stored in a loaded condition;
- a warning notice is posted wherever the explosive powered tool is being used.

A new aspect that has been brought into this regulation is that the issuing and collection of cartridges and nails or studs must be controlled and this control must be done in writing and be done by a person appointed in writing. There must be a register and the recipient must sign for receipt as must be done on return of equipment or cartridges etc.

Sub-regulation (3) deals with those issues that relate directly to the operator, in that he or she must be provided with eye protection, which must be worn, and that the operator must also be fully instructed, which indicates training in the operation, maintenance and use of such tools.

LCA Questions

1. Are all explosive powered tools provided with a protective guard around the muzzle?
2. Is the firing mechanism so designed that it will only fire if held against the surface at a force of twice its weight?
3. Is the firing mechanism so designed that the angle of inclination is not more than 15 degrees from the right angle when fired?
4. Are only cartridges that are suitable to explosive powered tools permitted to be used?
5. Are explosive tools cleaned at regular intervals?
6. Are explosive tools examined at regular intervals?
7. Are explosive tools and cartridges stored in a safe place?
8. Are explosive tools and cartridges stored in a place which is inaccessible to unauthorised persons?
9. Are the explosive powered tools stored in an unloaded position?
10. Are warning notices posted whenever explosive powered tools are in use?
11. Is the operator of such a tool provided with suitable eye protection?
12. Is the operator of such a tool instructed in the operation, maintenance and use of such tool?
13. Is the issuing of nails, cartridges or studs controlled and done in writing a person appointed in writing?
14. Is the issuing of nails, cartridges or studs recorded in a register signed by the recipient on receipt?

Regulation 20: Cranes

Notwithstanding the provisions of the Driven Machinery Regulations promulgated by Government Notice No. R.533 of 16 March 1990, as amended, a contractor shall ensure that where tower cranes are used—

(a) *account is taken of the effects of wind forces on the structure;*

(b) *account is taken of the bearing capacity of the ground on which the tower crane is to stand;*

(c) *the bases for the tower cranes and tracks for rail-mounted tower cranes are firm and level;*

(d) *the tower cranes are erected at a safe distance from excavations;*

(e) *there is sufficient clear space available for erection, operation and dismantling;*

(f) *the tower crane operators are competent to carry out the work safely; and*

(g) *the tower crane operators are physically and psychologically fit to work in such an environment by being in possession of a medical certificate of fitness.*

It is baffling as to why it was deemed necessary to address cranes in terms of these regulations as lifting machinery falls under the Driven Machinery Regulations and this regulation is referred to those regulations as well. The Driven machinery regulations should have been amended to address tower cranes.

However, this regulation requires that specific aspects be addressed in terms of tower cranes and these include the following

- The effects of wind forces
- The bearing capacity on the ground
- That the bases and rails be firm and level
- That they are erected at a safe distance from any excavations
- That there is sufficient clear space for erection, dismantling and operation
- That the operators are competent
- That the operators are physically and psychologically fit.

LCA Questions

1. Has the contractor ensured that when making use of tower cranes that the following are adhered to:
   - the effects of the wind forces on the structure are taken into consideration;
   - account is taken of the bearing capacity of the ground on which the tower is to stand;
   - the bases for the tower cranes and tracks for the rail mounted tower cranes are firm and level;
   - the tower cranes are erected a safe distance from excavations;
   - there is sufficient clear space available for erection, operation and dismantling;
   - operators are competent; and
   - operators are physically and psychological fit and in possession of a medical certificate of fitness?

Regulation 21: Construction vehicles and mobile plant

(1) A contractor shall ensure that all construction vehicles and mobile plants—

(a) are of an acceptable design and construction;

(b) are maintained in a good working order;

(c) are used in accordance with their design and the intention for which they where designed, having due regard to safety and health;

(d) are operated by workers who—

(i) have received appropriate training and been certified competent and been authorised to operate such machinery; and

(ii) are physically and psychologically fit to operate such construction vehicles and mobile plant by being in possession of a medical certificate of fitness;

(e) have safe and suitable means of access;

(f) are properly organised and controlled in any work situation by providing adequate signaling or other control arrangements to guard against the dangers relating to the movement of vehicles and plant, in order to ensure their continued safe operation;

(g) are prevented from falling into excavations, water or any other area lower than the working surface by installing adequate edge protection, which may include guardrails and crash barriers;

(h) where appropriate, are fitted with structures designed to protect the operator from falling material or from being crushed should the vehicle or mobile plant overturn;

(i) are equipped with an electrically operated acoustic signaling device and a reversing alarm; and

(j) are on a daily basis inspected prior to use, by a competent person who has been appointed in writing and the findings of such inspection is recorded in a register.

(2) A contractor shall furthermore ensure that—

(a) no person rides or be required or permitted to ride on any construction vehicle or mobile plant otherwise than in a safe place provided thereon for that purpose;

(b) every construction site is organised in such a way that, as far as is reasonably practicable, pedestrians and vehicles can move safely and without risks to health;

(c) the traffic routes are suitable for the persons using them, sufficient in number, in suitable positions and of sufficient size;

(d) every traffic route is, where necessary indicated by suitable signs for reasons of health or safety;

(e) all construction vehicles and mobile plant left unattended at night, adjacent to a freeway in normal use or adjacent to construction areas where work is in progress, shall have appropriate lights or reflectors, or barricades equipped with appropriate lights or reflectors, in order to identify the location of the vehicles or plant;

(f) bulldozers, scrapers, loaders, and other similar mobile plants are, when being repaired or when not in use, fully lowered or blocked with controls in a neutral position, motors stopped and brakes set;

(g) whenever visibility conditions warrant additional lighting, all mobile plants are equipped with at least two headlights and two taillights when in operation;

(h) tools and material are secured in order to prevent movement when transported in the same compartment with employees;

(i) vehicles used to transport employees have seats firmly secured and adequate for the number of employees to be carried; and

(j) when workers are working on or adjacent to public roads, reflective indicators are provided and worn by the workers.

Again this equipment is clearly defined as machinery and as such is largely addressed in terms of the machinery regulations. However there are a number of issues that have been included that need to be cleared up.

All operators have to be trained and certified as competent and must be physically and psychologically fit to carry out their functions.

The equipment must have safe and suitable means of access. The operation of such equipment must be organised and managed by means of signalling and any control measures that may be necessary to ensure their safe operation. Care must be taken to prevent such machinery from falling into excavations, water or areas lower than the area of operation. These precautionary measures would include barriers and guardrails etc.

The equipment must be fitted with devices to protect the operator should the equipment fall over or roll. This would include a cage or roll bars and together with this the appropriate seat belts.

This equipment must also have acoustic signalling devices and a reversing alarm.

This equipment must be inspected prior to use by a competent person who has been appointed in writing and the findings of the inspection must be recorded in a register.

No person other than the operator may ride on such equipment unless suitable safe seating is provided. Note that all vehicles used for the transport of employees must be fitted with adequately secured seating. During the operation of such equipment pedestrians and other vehicles must not be placed at risk. Suitable traffic routes must be demarcated together with suitable signage.

All construction vehicles that are left unattended at night or adjacent to a freeway or areas where work is being performed must have appropriate lights or reflectors or any means to identify the location of such equipment. Any equipment that a part can be raised must be left in the down position and the controls must be in neutral and blocked and the brakes fully applied.

When visibility conditions are poor or when operations are taking place at night the equipment must be fitted with at least two headlights and two taillights, which must be operational.

Although this has nothing to do with construction vehicles and mobile plant and is already addressed in General Safety Regulation 2, workers working adjacent or on public roads must wear reflective indicators at all times.

LCA Questions

1. Has the contractor ensured that all construction vehicles and mobile plant are of an acceptable design and construction and are used according to their design?
2. Are all construction vehicles and mobile plant maintained in good working order?
3. Is all construction and mobile equipment operated by workers who have been trained and certified as competent.
4. Are all construction and mobile equipment operated by workers who have been declared fit physically and psychologically?
5. Do all construction vehicles and mobile equipment have safe and suitable means of access?
6. Are all construction vehicles and mobile plant properly organised and is there a method of signals in place?
7. Are all construction vehicles and mobile plant prevented from falling into excavations, water or any other area lower than the working area by installing adequate edge protection?
8. Are the operators of construction vehicles and mobile plant protected from falling material or from being crushed in the case of the vehicle rolling?
9. Are all construction vehicles and mobile equipment fitted with electric ally operated acoustic signalling devices and a reversing alarm?
10. Are all construction vehicles inspected daily prior to use, by an appointed competent person and is the inspection recorded in a register?

11. Are persons only permitted to ride in a construction vehicle when in a safe position provided for this purpose?
12. Are pedestrians on construction sites adequately protected?
13. Are there sufficient and suitable traffic routes on site?
14. Are there sufficient and suitable traffic signs on the construction site?
15. Are all construction vehicles and mobile plant that is left unattended at night so fitted with appropriate lights or reflectors so that they can easily by identified?
16. Are all bulldozers, scrapers, loaders and other similar mobile plants, when being repaired or when not in use, fully lowered or blocked with controls in a neutral position, motors stopped and brakes set?
17. When visibility is poor are all construction vehicles and mobile plant fitted with at least two headlights and two taillights when in operation?
18. When tools and materials are transported together with employees are such tools and materials firmly secured to prevent movement?
19. Are all vehicles used to transport employees fitted with fixed seats of adequate number for the employees being transported?
20. When employees are working adjacent to or on public roads are they supplied with and required to wear reflective indicators?

Regulation 22: Electrical installations and machinery on construction sites

Notwithstanding the provisions contained in the Electrical Installation Regulations promulgated by Government Notice No. R.2920 of 23 October 1992 and the Electrical Machinery Regulations promulgated by Government Notice No. R.1953 of 12 August 1988, respectively, as amended, a contractor shall ensure that—

(a) before construction commences and during the progress thereof, adequate steps are taken to ascertain the presence of and guard against danger to workers from any electrical cable or apparatus which is under, over or on the site;

(b) all parts of electrical installations and machinery are of adequate strength to withstand the working conditions on construction sites;

(c) in working areas where the exact location of underground electric power lines is unknown, employees using jackhammers, shovels or other hand tools which may make contact with a power line, are provided with insulated protective gloves or otherwise that the handle of the tool being used is insulated;

(d) all temporary electrical installations are inspected at least once a week and electrical machinery on a daily basis before use on a construction site by competent persons and the records of these inspections are recorded in a register to be kept on site; and

(e) the control of all temporary electrical installations on the construction site is designated to a competent person who has been appointed in writing.

Although the electrical aspects are adequately addressed in terms of the electrical installations and they must also be complied with the legislature has also addressed other aspect that are important.

The contractor must before construction commences and during the progress take steps to guard against any dangers that may arise from any electrical cables or apparatus on site. All electrical installation must be able to withstand the conditions on a construction site. The exact location of all cable must be established and employees working with jackhammers etc. must be protected by means of adequate insulation.

All temporary installations must be inspected once a week and electrical machinery must be inspected daily before use. This inspection must be done by a competent person and be recorded into a register. The question that arises in this case is who would be regarded as being competent. It may be difficult to establish the competency of a person in this case who is not a qualified electrician and if such person is used his competency will have to be confirmed by an inspector in terms of General Machinery Regulation 5. This could mean that an electrician will have to be employed or a contractor appointed on all construction sites. This is also because control by a competent person must also be exercised on all temporary installations.

LCA Questions

1. Has the contractor ensured that before construction commences and during the progress thereof, adequate steps are taken to establish the presence of and guard against any danger to the workers in respect to electrical cables or apparatus?
2. Are all electrical installations and machinery strong enough to withstand the working conditions?
3. In those areas where it cannot be established where electrical devices are, have the employees working with tools that could come into contact with such devices, been protected by means of rubber insulated gloves or insulating the handle of the tool?
4. Are all temporary electrical installation been inspected at least once a week by a competent person and are such inspection recorded?
5. Is all electrical machinery inspected daily by a competent person and is such inspection recorded?
6. Has the control of a temporary electrical installation on a construction site been designated to an appointed competent person?

Regulation 23: Use and temporary storage of flammable liquids on construction sites

Notwithstanding the provisions for the use and storage of flammable liquids as determined in the General Safety Regulations promulgated by Government Notice No. R.1031 dated 30 May 1986, as amended, a contractor shall ensure that—

(a) where flammable liquids are being used, applied or stored at the workplace concerned, this is done in such a manner which would cause no fire or explosion hazard, and that the workplace is effectively ventilated: Provided that where the workplace cannot effectively be ventilated—

(i) every employee involved is provided with a respirator, mask or breathing apparatus of a type approved by the chief inspector, and

(ii) steps are taken to ensure that every such employee, while using or applying flammable liquid, uses the apparatus supplied to him or her;

(b) *no person smokes in any place in which flammable liquid is used or stored, and such contractor shall affix a suitable and conspicuous notice at all entrances to any such areas prohibiting such smoking;*

(c) *flammable liquids on a construction site is stored in a well-ventilated reasonably fire resistant container, cage or room and kept locked with proper access control measures in place;*

(d) *an adequate amount of efficient fire-fighting equipment is installed in suitable locations around the flammable liquids store with the recognized symbolic signs;*

(e) *only the quantity of flammable liquid needed for work on one day is to be taken out of the store for use;*

(f) *all containers holding flammable liquids are kept tightly closed when not in actual use and, after their contents have been used up, to be removed from the construction site and safely disposed of;*

(g) *where flammable liquids are decanted, the metal containers are bonded or earthed; and*

(h) *no flammable material such as cotton waste, paper, cleaning rags or similar material is stored together with flammable liquids.*

This regulation is not necessary and does not make anymore requirements as to what is already required in terms of the General Safety Regulations and also The Regulations for Hazardous Chemical Substances. It is for this reason that no further comment is required in terms of this regulation.

LCA Questions

1. Have all flammable liquids used on a construction site been stored in such a manner that they would not cause any fire or explosion and are adequately ventilated?
2. Are all employees working with flammable liquids been provided with and use the appropriate PPE?
3. In those instances where flammable liquids are used are persons prohibited from smoking and is signage accordingly posted?
4. Are all flammable liquids on a construction site kept locked in an appropriate reasonably fire resistant container, cage or room and is access control exercised?
5. Is adequate fire fighting equipment provided with adequate and appropriate signage?
6. Are all containers holding flammable liquids kept tightly closed and are empties removed off site?
7. Is only the amount of flammable liquid required for one days work removed from the storage facility at any time?
8. Where flammable liquids are decanted have the container into which and from which they are being decanted been bonded and earthed?
9. Have steps been taken to ensure that no flammable material such as cotton waste, paper, cleaning rags etc are stored with flammable liquids?

Regulation 24: Water environments

(1) A contractor shall ensure that where construction work is done over or in close proximity to water, provision is made for—

(a) preventing workers from falling into water; and

(b) the rescuing of workers in danger of drowning.

(2) A contractor shall ensure that where a worker is exposed to the risk of drowning by falling into the water, a lifejacket is provided to and worn by the worker.

This has been a regulations that has been long in coming unfortunately it should be in a more general set of regulations such as the General Safety Regulations because the impression that is being created is that this regulation is only applicable to a construction site. Should an incident ever occur involving a water environment an inspector would most probably first have to prove that construction work was in fact being done. It is recommended that all employers implement the requirements of this regulation.

Steps must be taken to prevent persons from falling into water and also for the rescuing of persons that are drowning. All persons exposed to the risk of drowning must be issued with and be required to wear a lifejacket.

LCA Questions

1. Where work is carried out over or near water has the contractor ensured that:
   - provision is made to prevent workers from falling into the water;
   - provision is made to rescue workers in danger of drowning?
2. Where a worker is at risk of falling into water has the contractor provided such worker with a life jacket?

Regulation 25: Housekeeping on construction sites

Notwithstanding the provisions of the Environmental Regulations for Workplaces promulgated by Government Notice No. R.2281 dated 16 October 1987, as amended, a contractor shall ensure that—

(a) suitable housekeeping is continuously implemented on each construction site, including provisions for the—

(i) proper storage of materials and equipment, and

(ii) removal of scrap, waste and debris at appropriate intervals;

(b) loose materials required for use, are not placed or allowed to accumulate on the site so as to obstruct means of access to and egress from workplaces and passageways;

(c) waste and debris are not disposed of from a high place with a chute, unless the chute complies with the requirements set out regulation 12 (6);

(d) construction sites in built-up areas, adjacent to a public way, are suitably and sufficiently fenced off and provided with controlled access points to prevent the entry of unauthorized persons;

(e) a catch platform or net is erected above an entrance or passageway or above a place where persons work or pass under, or fence off the danger area if work is

being performed above such entrance, passageway, or place so as to ensure that all persons are kept safe in the case of danger or possibility of persons being struck by falling objects.

Again this regulation is adequately addressed in terms of regulation 6 of the Environment Regulations for Workplaces and is self-explanatory.

LCA Questions

1. Has suitable housekeeping been continuously implemented on site providing for proper storage of materials and equipment and the removal of scrap and waste?
2. Have steps been taken to ensure that loose material need for use is not allowed to accumulate so as to obstruct means of access to and egress from the workplace?
3. Is the construction site that is adjacent to build up areas, public way sufficiently fenced off and provided with controlled access points to prevent unauthorised entry onto the site?
4. In those instances where there is a danger of falling objects striking persons have catch nets been erected?

Regulation 26: Stacking and storage on construction sites

Notwithstanding the provisions for the stacking of articles contained in the General Safety Regulations promulgated by Government Notice No. R.1031 dated 30 May 1986, as amended, a contractor shall ensure that—

(a) a competent person is appointed in writing with the duty of supervising all stacking and storage on a construction site;

(b) adequate storage areas are provided;

(c) there are demarcated storage areas; and

(d) storage areas are kept neat and under control.

This regulation too is adequately addressed in terms of the General Safety Regulation 8 and is also self-explanatory and needs no further comment. The need to have included this into these regulations does not make sense as nothing new or specific is addressed.

LCA Questions

1. Has the contractor appointed in writing a competent person to supervise all stacking and storage on site?
2. Has the contractor ensured that there is adequate storage areas provided on site?
3. Has the contractor ensured that the storage areas are clearly demarcated?
4. Has the contractor ensured that storage areas are kept neat and under control?

Regulation 27: Fire precautions on construction sites

Subject to the provisions of the Environmental Regulations for Workplaces promulgated by Government Notice No. R.2281 of 16 October 1987, as amended, every contractor shall ensure that—

(a) all appropriate measures are taken to avoid the risk of fire;

(b) *sufficient and suitable storage is provided for flammable liquids, solids and gases;*

(c) *smoking is prohibited and notices in this regard are prominently displayed in all places containing readily combustible or flammable materials;*

(d) *in confined spaces and other places in which flammable gases, vapours or dust can cause danger—*

(i) *only suitably protected electrical installations and equipment, including portable lights, are used;*

(ii) *there are no flames or similar means of ignition;*

(iii) *there are conspicuous notices prohibiting smoking;*

(iv) *oily rags, waste and other substances liable to ignite are without delay removed to a safe place; and*

(v) *adequate ventilation is provided;*

(e) *combustible materials do not accumulate on the construction site;*

(f) *welding, flame cutting and other hot work are done only after the appropriate precautions as required have been taken to reduce the risk of fire;*

(g) *suitable and sufficient fire-extinguishing equipment is placed at strategic locations or as may be recommended by the Fire Chief or local authority concerned, and that such equipment is maintained in a good working order;*

(h) *the fire equipment contemplated in paragraph (g) is inspected by a competent person, who has been appointed in writing, in the manner indicated by the manufacturer thereof;*

(i) *a sufficient number of workers are trained in the use of fire- extinguishing equipment;*

(j) *where appropriate, suitable visual signs are provided to clearly indicate the escape routes in the case of a fire;*

(k) *the means of escape is kept clear at all times;*

(l) *there is an effective evacuation plan providing for all—*

(i) *persons to be evacuated speedily without panic;*

(ii) *persons to be accounted for; and*

(iii) *plant and processes to be shut down; and*

(m) *a siren is installed and sounded in the event of a fire.*

Although this aspect is addressed in terms of two regulations those being The Environmental Regulations for Workplaces and the Vessels Under Pressure Regulations certain further aspects have been included.

These aspects are that suitable fire fighting extinguishers must be suitably placed and this is going to create a problem due to theft and is going to be difficult to manage. Reference is made to the extinguishers being inspected by a competent person and there was no need for this as it is specifically addressed in terms of the Vessels Under Pressure Regulations. Person needs to be trained in the use of these extinguishers and signage where appropriate to be posted indicating escape routes.

An evacuation plan has to be drawn up and be implemented. This is not addressed anywhere other than in the Major Hazard Installation Regulations and this too should have been placed in a more general regulations such the Environmental Regulations for Workplaces.

LCA Questions

1. Has the contractor ensured that:
   - all appropriate steps are taken to avoid the risk of fire;
   - sufficient and suitable storage is provided for flammable liquids, solids and gases;
   - smoking is prohibited and notices posted; and
   - precautions in respect of confined spaces are adhered to?
2. Does the contractor ensure that combustible material does not accumulate on site?
3. Does the contractor ensure that when hot work is carried out are fire precautions taken?
4. Does the contractor ensure that suitable and sufficient fire fighting equipment is placed in strategic positions?
5. Does the contractor ensure that fire fighting equipment is inspected by an appointed competent person?
6. Has the contractor ensured that a sufficient number of employees have been trained in the use of fire fighting equipment?
7. Has the contractor ensured that appropriate and suitable signs indicating escape routes have been posted?
8. Has the contractor ensured that escape routes are kept clear?
9. Has the contractor ensured that there is an effective evacuation plan in place?
10. Does the evacuation plan ensure that persons can be speedily evacuated without panic, that all persons are accounted for and that plant and processes are shut down?
11. Has the contractor ensured that a siren has been installed and can be sounded in the event of a fire?

Regulation 28: Construction welfare facilities

(1) Notwithstanding the construction site provisions contained in the Facilities Regulations promulgated by Government Notice No. R.1593 of 12 August 1988, as amended, a contractor shall, depending on the number of workers and the duration of the work, provide at or within reasonable access of every construction site, the following clean and maintained facilities:

(a) at least one shower facility for every 15 workers;

(b) at least one sanitary facility for every 30 workers;

(c) changing facilities for each sex; and

(d) sheltered eating areas.

(2) A contractor shall provide reasonable and suitable living accommodation for the workers at construction sites which are remote from their homes and where adequate transportation between the site and their homes, or other suitable living accommodation, is not available.

This regulation is also largely addressed by the Facility Regulations and very little extra is addressed here. This regulation stipulates that a construction site must have shower facilities for every 15 workers, which is very seldom found on building sites and could be a problem. Toilet facilities are not a major issue and are normally addressed by chemical toilets.

What is new is that a contractor must provide suitable accommodation when doing work away from their base station. This regulation does not require accommodation in general to be provided as some people may think.

LCA Questions

1. Has the contractor provide the following:
   - at least one shower for every 15 workers;
   - at least one sanitary facility for every 30 workers;
   - a changing facility for each sex; and
   - sheltered eating areas?
2. In those instances where the construction site is in a remote area has the contractor provided suitable living accommodation facilities?

Regulation 29: Approved inspection authorities

(1) The Chief Inspector may approve as an Inspection Authority any organization that has been accredited in terms of the provision of the Act and these regulations.

(2) The Chief Inspector may at any time withdraw any approval of an approved inspection authority, subject to section 35 of the Act.

It is interesting as to why the legislature deemed it necessary include this regulation with respect to approved inspection authorities. It serves no purpose to approve inspection authorities if there is no task for them to carry out. Nowhere in the regulations other than in this regulation is any reference made to approved inspection authorities. It may well be that the legislature at some future stage may place duties on the employer or contractor to make use of approved inspection authorities.

Regulation 30: Offences and penalties

Any person who contravenes or fails to comply with any of the provisions of regulations 3, 4, 5, 6, 7, 8, 9, 10, 11, 12, 13, 14, 15, 16, 17, 18, 19, 20, 21, 22, 23, 24, 25, 26, 27 and 28, shall be guilty of an offence and liable upon conviction to a fine or to imprisonment for a maximum of 12 months and, in the case of a continuous offence, to an additional fine of R200 for each day on which the offence continues or additional imprisonment of one day for each day on which the offence continues: Provided that the period of such additional imprisonment shall not exceed 90 days.

Regulation 13A of the General Safety Regulations: Ladders

(1) An employer shall ensure that every ladder is constructed of sound material and is suitable for the purpose for which it is used, and—

(a) is fitted with non-skid devices at the bottom ends and hooks or similar devices at the upper ends of the stiles which shall ensure the stability of the ladder during normal use; or

(b) *is so lashed, held or secured whilst being used as to ensure the stability of the ladder under all conditions and at all times.*

(2) No employer shall use a ladder, or permit it to be used, if it—

(a) *(i) has rungs fastened to the stiles only by means of nails, screws, spikes or in like manner; or*

(ii) has rungs which have not been properly let into the stiles: Provided that in the case of welded ladders or ladders of which the rungs are bolted or rivetted to the stiles, the rungs need not be let into the stiles; or

(b) *has damaged stiles, or damaged or missing rungs.*

(3) No employer may permit that—

(a) *a ladder which is required to be leaned against an object for support be used which is longer than 9 m; and*

(b) *except with the approval of an inspector, the reach of a ladder be extended by fastening together two or more ladders:*

Provided that the provisions of this subregulation shall not apply to extension or free-standing ladders.

(4) In the case of wooden ladders the employer shall ensure that—

(a) *the ladders are constructed of straight grained wood, free from defects, and with the grain running in the length of the stiles and rungs; and*

(b) *the ladders are not painted or covered in any manner, unless it has been established that there are no cracks or other inherent weaknesses: Provided that ladders may be treated with oil or covered with clear varnish or wood preservative.*

(5) When work is done from a ladder, the employer shall—

(a) *take special precautionary measures to prevent articles from falling off; and*

(b) *provide suitable sheaths or receptacles in which handtools shall be kept when not being used.*

(6) An employer shall ensure that a fixed ladder which exceeds 5 m in length and is attached to a vertical structure with an inclination to the horizontal level of 75° or more—

(a) *has its rungs at least 150 mm away from the structure to which the ladder is attached; and*

(b) *is provided with a cage which—*

(i) extends from a point not exceeding 2,5 m from the lower level to a height of at least 900 mm above the top level served by the ladder; and

(ii) shall afford firm support along its whole length for the back of the person climbing the ladder, and for which purpose no part of the cage shall be more than 700 mm away from the level of the rungs:

Provided that the foregoing provisions of paragraph (b) shall not apply if platforms, which are spaced not more than 8 m apart and suitable for persons to rest on, are provided.

This regulation is to a large extent self-explanatory. It is important that regulation 13(A) be read thoroughly.

Note that nowhere in this regulation is it stipulated that inspections must be carried out or that a record of any inspections must be kept. However, in terms of section 8 of the Act it is required that the risks be assessed and reduced or removed where necessary and the ladders must be assessed in order to comply. This would have to be done on a regular basis.

The proviso in sub-regulation 6 appears to be totally contrary to the requirements of sub-regulations 6 (a) and (b) with respect to the cage. Although the proviso may be badly written, it was originally intended to include only those ladders which were within a lattice work of no more than one meter wide. This makes it easier to understand why the proviso was included. Note that it is intended that this issue be addressed when these regulations are amended.

Conclusion

As has been said the intention of these regulations is good, but it is going to take some policing not only by inspectors but by the client, principal contractor and contractors. If there is commitment and these regulations are fully implemented and largely complied with there should be a substantial reduction in terms of the incidents that take place in the construction industry.

Annexures

ANNEXURE A

NOTIFICATION OF CONSTRUCTION WORK
Regulation 3 of the Construction Regulations, 2003

1. (*a*) Name and postal address of principal contractor:

   ....

   (*b*) Name and telephone number of principal contractor's contact person:

   ....

2. Principal contractor's compensation registration number:

   ....

3. (*a*) Name and postal address of client:

   ....

   (*b*) Name and telephone number of client's contact person or agent:

   ....

4. (*a*) Name and postal address of designer(*s*) for the project:

   ....

   (*b*) Name and telephone number of designer's contact person:

   ....

5. Name and telephone number of principal contractor's construction supervisor on site appointed in terms of regulations 6 (1):

   ....

6. Name/s of principal contractor's sub-ordinate supervisors on site appointed in terms of regulation 6 (2):

   ....

7. Exact physical address of the contruction site or site office:

   ....

8. Nature of the construction work:

   ....

   ....

   ....

9. Expected commencement date: ....

10. Expected completion date: ....

11. Estimated maximum numer of persons on the construction site:

    ....

12. Planned number of contractors on the construction site accountable to principal contractor:

    ....

13. Name(*s*) of contractors already chosen:

    ....

    ....

    ....

....

Principal Contractor *Date*

....

Client *Date*

- THIS DOCUMENT IS TO BE FORWARDED TO THE OFFICE OF THE DEPARTMENT OF LABOUR **PRIOR TO COMMENCEMENT** OF WORK ON SITE.
- **ALL PRINCIPAL CONTRACTORS** THAT QUALIFY TO NOTIFY MUST DO SO EVEN IF ANOTHER PRINCIPAL CONTRACTOR ON THE SAME SITE HAD DONE SO PRIOR TO THE COMMENCEMENT OF WORK.

ANNEXURE B

GENERAL ADMINISTRATIVE TEMPLATES

COMPANY NAME/LOGO

SITE ADDRESS

HEALTH AND SAFETY COMMITTEE

AGENDA

1. Matters arising from previous minutes.
2. Health and Safety deviation reports.
3. Incidents.
4. General.
   4.1 ______________________
   4.2 ______________________
   4.3 ______________________
   4.4 ______________________
   4.5 ______________________
5. Date of next meeting: ______________________

COMPANY NAME/LOGO

SITE ADDRESS

HEALTH AND SAFETY COMMITTEE

MEETING MINUTES

MEETING NUMBER: ____________________

DATE: ____________________

TIME STARTED: ____________________

TIME ADJOURNED: ____________________

PRESENT:

1. ________	2. ________	3. ________
4. ________	5. ________	6. ________
7. ________	8. ________	9. ________
10. ________	11. ________	11 ________

ABSENT:

1. ________	2. ________	3. ________
4. ________	5. ________	6. ________
7. ________	8. ________	9. ________

CONFIRM MINUTES OF MEETING No: ____________________ **DATED:** ____________________

1. MATTERS ARISING FROM PREVIOUS MINUTES	**Action by**	**Completion Date**
2. HEALTH & SAFETY REPRESENTATIVES DEVIATION REPORT		

3. INCIDENTS	**Action by**	**Completion Date**
Name: Date:		
Description:		
Cause of incident:		
Preventative action:		
Name: Date:		
Description:		
Cause of incident:		
Preventative action:		
Name: Date:		
Description:		
Cause of incident:		
Preventative action:		
Name: Date:		
Description:		
Cause of incident:		
Preventative action:		

4. GENERAL	**Action by**	**Completion Date**
Health and safety to pick for the meeting (E.g. housekeeping, vehicles etc):		
Health and safety suggestions:		
Off-the-job health and safety topic of the month:		
Other matters		
Date of next meeting:		

Signature Chairman:	**Date:**
Signature Employer:	**Date:**

COMPANY NAME/LOGO

SITE ADDRESS

HEALTH AND SAFETY REPRESENTATIVE

ELECTION FORM

DEPARTMENT: ....

DATE: ....

1. ☐
2. ☐
3. ☐
4. ☐
5. ☐
6. ☐

Kindly note that the appointment of a health and safety representative is a serious contribution to the health and safety system within the company. It is for this reason that careful consideration must be given when electing the health and safety representative. Ensure that the person you elect is in your mind the most competent person for the task.

PLEASE ENSURE THAT YOU MARK ONLY ONE NAME WITH AN X. THE MARKING OF MORE THAN ONE NAME WILL RESULT IN THE BALLOT PAPER HAVING TO BE DESTROYED.

COMPANY NAME/LOGO

SITE ADDRESS

HEALTH AND SAFETY REPRESENTATIVE

NOMINATION FORM

DEPARTMENT: ....

DATE: ....

1. ....
2. ....
3. ....
4. ....
5. ....
6. ....

Kindly note that the appointment of a health and safety representative is a serious contribution to the health and safety system within the company. It is for this reason that when making a nomination it is vitally important that you ensure that the person who is nominated will be competent to carry out the tasks required of a health and safety representative and that such person will be committed to the position.

Note also, that the person nominated must be a full time employee and must be familiar with the area for which he or she is nominated.

PLEASE ENSURE THAT YOU PRINT THE NAME OF YOUR NOMINEE CLEARLY TOGETHER WITH THE INITIALS OF THE INDIVIDUAL NOMINATED.

ANNEXURE C

APPOINTMENT LETTERS

COMPANY NAME/LOGO

SITE ADDRESS

OCCUPATIONAL HEALTH AND SAFETY ACT, 1993

SECTION 17 – HEALTH AND SAFETY REPRESENTATIVE APPOINTMENT

APPOINTEE'S NAME

I, Appointer's Full Name the Legislative reference of appointment appointee of Area of responsibility hereby appoint you Appointee's Full Name in terms of Section 17 as the Health and Safety Representative for Area of responsibility.

In terms of this appointment the following are your functions:

1. To represent your employee electorate's interests in terms of occupational health and safety.
2. Carry out health and safety inspections of your workplace as designated above prior to the health and safety committee meeting.
3. Serve on the appropriate health and safety committee.
4. Bring to the attention of your supervisor any deviations in respect to health and safety that come to your attention.

Dates and times of health and safety committee meetings will be determined by the committee. Such meetings as determined by the committee should be attended.

You will be required to undergo Health and Safety Representative training in order to ensure that you can complete your tasks successfully.

Your appointment is valid from Start Date to End Date

....

Appointer's Full Name

....

Date

ACCEPTANCE

I, Appointee's Full Name understand the implications of the appointment as detailed above and confirm my acceptance.

....

Appointee's Full Name

....

Date

PLACE COMPANY/LOGO

COMPANY NAME

COMPANY ADDRESS

OCCUPATIONAL HEALTH AND SAFETY ACT, ACT 85 OF 1993

CONSTRUCTION REGULATION 4 (1) (c)

APPOINTMENT OF THE PRINCIPAL CONTRACTOR

PRINCIPAL CONTRACTOR'S NAME

I, client's name hereby appoint principal contractors name as the principal contractor responsible for site address to carry out the construction work of description of construction work and if more than one principal contractor area of responsibility.

You shall ensure that you meet all the requirements in terms of the Act and in particular in terms of the Construction Regulations. You shall also ensure that all contractors appointed by yourself and reporting to you comply with the requirements as stipulated in the Construction Regulations.

You shall also ensure that all the information and specifications to ensure that the construction work is carried out in a safe manner are carried over to all contractors appointed and reporting to you.

You shall further ensure that all records, registers and required lists are maintained and that all persons appointed to carry out tasks as stipulated by these regulations are competent and have the necessary resources to complete their tasks effectively in such a manner that health and safety is not in any manner compromised.

This appointment is valid from date to co the completion of the stipulated construction work.

You shall submit a written weekly report on all shortfalls that have not been met in terms of these regulations.

....	....
Client's full name	Date

Kindly confirm your acceptance of this appointment by completing the following:

I, principal contractor understand the implications of the appointment as detailed above and confirm my acceptance.

....	....
Principal contractor's full name	Date

PLACE COMPANY LOGO

COMPANY NAME

COMPANY ADDRESS

OCCUPATIONAL HEALTH AND SAFETY ACT, ACT 85 OF 1993

CONSTRUCTION REGULATION 4 (5)

APPOINTMENT OF THE CLIENT AGENT

CLIENT'S AGENT'S NAME

I, client's name hereby appoint agents name as the agent responsible for site address to manage the construction work of description of construction work.

You shall ensure that all the requirements in terms of the Act and in particular in terms of the Construction Regulations are met. You shall also ensure that all appointed contractors comply with the requirements as stipulated in the Construction Regulations.

You shall also ensure that all the information and specifications to ensure that the construction work is carried out in a safe manner are carried over to all appointed contractors.

You shall further ensure that all records, registers and required lists are maintained and shall stop construction work upon identifying any non-compliance by any contractors; this includes stopping any work should the competency of the person carrying out such work be questionable.

This appointment is valid from date to the completion of the stipulated construction work.

....

Client's full name Date

Kindly confirm your acceptance of this appointment by completing the following:

I, agents name understand the implications of the appointment as detailed above and confirm my acceptance.

....

Agent's full name Date

PLACE COMPANY LOGO

COMPANY NAME

COMPANY ADDRESS

OCCUPATIONAL HEALTH AND SAFETY ACT, ACT 85 OF 1993

CONSTRUCTION REGULATION 5 (3) (b)

APPOINTMENT OF THE CONTRACTOR

CONTRACTOR'S NAME

I, principal contractor/contractor name hereby appoint contractors name as the contractor responsible for site address to carry out the construction work of description of construction work.

You shall ensure that you meet all the requirements in terms of the Act and in particular in terms of the Construction Regulations. You shall also ensure that all contractors appointed by yourself and reporting to you comply with the requirements as stipulated in the Construction Regulations.

You shall also ensure that all the information and specifications to ensure that the construction work is carried out in a safe manner are carried over to all contractors appointed and reporting to you.

You shall further ensure that all records, registers and required lists are maintained and that all persons appointed to carry out tasks as stipulated by these regulations are competent and have the necessary resources to complete their tasks effectively in such a manner that health and safety is not in any manner compromised.

This appointment is valid from date to the completion of the stipulated construction work.

You shall submit a written weekly report on all shortfalls that have not been met in terms of these regulations.

....

Principal contractor's/contractor's full name Date

Kindly confirm your acceptance of this appointment by completing the following:

I, contractor name understand the implications of the appointment as detailed above and confirm my acceptance.

....

Contractor's full name Date

PLACE COMPANY LOGO

COMPANY NAME

COMPANY ADDRESS

OCCUPATIONAL HEALTH AND SAFETY ACT, ACT 85 OF 1993

CONSTRUCTION REGULATION 6 (1)

APPOINTMENT OF THE CONSTRUCTION SUPERVISOR

CONSTRUCTION SUPERVISOR'S NAME

I, principal contractor/contractor name hereby appoint construction supervisor's name as the supervisor responsible for site address to carry out the construction work of description of construction work and area of responsibility.

In terms of this appointment you are required to ensure that all construction work performed under your supervision is carried out as follows:

1. By persons suitably trained and competent to do such work;
2. That all statutory appointments have been completed;
3. That, where required, health and safety committees are established and that meetings are accordingly held;
4. That all persons are aware and understand the hazards attached to the work being carried out;
5. That the required risk assessments are carried out;
6. That precautionary measures are identified and implemented;
7. That discipline is enforced at the construction site at all times;
8. That all identified statutory requirements are met; and
9. That any other interests in terms of health and safety with respect to the responsible area are met.

You are required to report any deviations of the above-mentioned instructions to contractor's name.

This appointment is valid from date to the completion of the stipulated construction work.

You shall submit a written weekly report on all shortfalls that have not been met in terms of these regulations.

....

Principal contractor's/contractor's full name Date

Kindly confirm your acceptance of this appointment by completing the following:

I, construction supervisor understand the implications of the appointment as detailed above and confirm my acceptance.

....

Construction supervisor's full name Date

PLACE COMPANY LOGO

COMPANY NAME

COMPANY ADDRESS

OCCUPATIONAL HEALTH AND SAFETY ACT, ACT 85 OF 1993

CONSTRUCTION REGULATION 6 (2)

APPOINTMENT OF THE ASSISTANT CONSTRUCTION SUPERVISOR

ASSISTANT CONSTRUCTION SUPERVISOR'S NAME

I, principal contractor/contractor name hereby appoint assistant construction supervisor's name as the assistant supervisor responsible for site address to carry out the construction work of description of construction work and area of responsibility.

In terms of this appointment you are required to ensure that all construction work performed under your supervision is carried out as follows:

1. By persons suitably trained and competent to do such work;
2. That all statutory appointments have been completed;
3. That, where required, health and safety committees are established and that meetings are accordingly held;
4. That all persons are aware and understand the hazards attached to the work being carried out;
5. That the required risk assessments are carried out;
6. That precautionary measures are identified and implemented;
7. That discipline is enforced at the construction site at all times;
8. That all identified statutory requirements are met; and
9. That any other interests in terms of health and safety with respect to the responsible area are met.

You are required to report any deviations of the above-mentioned instructions to construction supervisor's name.

This appointment is valid from date to the completion of the stipulated construction work.

You shall submit a written weekly report on all shortfalls that have not been met in terms of these regulations.

....

Principal contractor's/contractor's full name Date

Kindly confirm your acceptance of this appointment by completing the following:

I, assistant construction supervisor understand the implications of the appointment as detailed above and confirm my acceptance.

....

Assistant construction supervisor's full name Date

PLACE COMPANY LOGO

COMPANY NAME

COMPANY ADDRESS

OCCUPATIONAL HEALTH AND SAFETY ACT, ACT 85 OF 1993

CONSTRUCTION REGULATION 6 (6)

APPOINTMENT OF THE CONSTRUCTION SITE HEALTH AND SAFETY OFFICER

HEALTH AND SAFETY OFFICER'S NAME

I, contractor's name hereby appoint safety officer's name as the construction site health and safety officer responsible for site address to manage all the health and safety issues as required in terms of the Act.

You shall ensure that all the requirements in terms of the Act and in particular in terms of the Construction Regulations are met. You shall also ensure that all appointed contractors comply with the requirements as stipulated in the Construction Regulations.

You shall further ensure that all records, registers and required lists are maintained and shall stop construction work upon identifying any non-compliance by any contractors; this includes stopping any work should the competency of the person carrying out such work be questionable.

This appointment is valid from date to the completion of the stipulated construction work.

....

Contractors full name Date

Kindly confirm your acceptance of this appointment by completing the following:

I, construction site health and safety officer's name understand the implications of the appointment as detailed above and confirm my acceptance.

....

Construction site health and safety officer's full name Date

PLACE COMPANY LOGO

COMPANY NAME

COMPANY ADDRESS

OCCUPATIONAL HEALTH AND SAFETY ACT, ACT 85 OF 1993

CONSTRUCTION REGULATION 7 (1)

APPOINTMENT OF THE CONSTRUCTION SITE RISK ASSESSOR

RISK ASSESSOR'S NAME

I, contractor's name hereby appoint risk assessor's name as the construction site risk assessor responsible for site address to carry out risk assessments prior to the commencement of construction work and any other risk assessment that may be required for the duration of the construction work.

You shall ensure that all risks are identified and analyzed and that safe working procedures are drafted and implemented to reduce, mitigate or controls the hazards that were identified.

This appointment is valid from date to the completion of the stipulated construction work.

....

Contractor's full name Date

Kindly confirm your acceptance of this appointment by completing the following:

I, construction site risk assessor's name understand the implications of the appointment as detailed above and confirm my acceptance.

....

Construction site risk assessor's full name Date

PLACE COMPANY LOGO

COMPANY NAME

COMPANY ADDRESS

OCCUPATIONAL HEALTH AND SAFETY ACT, ACT 85 OF 1993

CONSTRUCTION REGULATION 8 (1) (a)

APPOINTMENT OF THE FALL PROTECTION PLAN DEVELOPER

FALL PROTECTION PLAN DEVELOPER'S NAME

I, principal contractor/contractor name hereby appoint fall protection plan developer's name as the fall protection plan developer responsible for site address to develop a fall protection plan and ensure it implementation.

You shall ensure that you meet all the requirements in terms of the Construction Regulations in terms of the fall protection plan. You shall also ensure that all persons are trained on the fall protection plan and that such plan is at all times implemented.

This appointment is valid from date to the completion of the stipulated construction work.

....

Principal contractor's/contractor's full name Date

Kindly confirm your acceptance of this appointment by completing the following:

I, fall protection plan developer's full name understand the implications of the appointment as detailed above and confirm my acceptance.

....

Fall protection plan developer's full name Date

PLACE COMPANY LOGO

COMPANY NAME

COMPANY ADDRESS

OCCUPATIONAL HEALTH AND SAFETY ACT, ACT 85 OF 1993

CONSTRUCTION REGULATION 10 (a)

APPOINTMENT OF THE FORMWORK AND SUPPORT WORK SUPERVISOR

FORMWORK AND SUPPORT WORK SUPERVISOR'S NAME

I, principal contractor/contractor name hereby appoint formwork and support work supervisor's name as the formwork and support work supervisor responsible for site address to supervise and carry out all the necessary inspections in terms of all formwork and support work.

You shall ensure that when becoming aware of any health and safety hazards in respect to formwork and support work that the necessary precautionary measures are taken and enforced.

You shall further ensure that the requirements of the Construction Regulations are at all times met. On identifying any shortfalls or hazards convey such information in writing to the construction supervisor.

This appointment is valid from date to the completion of the stipulated construction work.

....

Principal contractor's/contractor's full name Date

Kindly confirm your acceptance of this appointment by completing the following:

I, formwork and support work supervisor's full name understand the implications of the appointment as detailed above and confirm my acceptance.

....

Formwork and support work supervisor's full name Date

PLACE COMPANY LOGO

COMPANY NAME

COMPANY ADDRESS

OCCUPATIONAL HEALTH AND SAFETY ACT, ACT 85 OF 1993

CONSTRUCTION REGULATION 11 (1)

APPOINTMENT OF THE EXCAVATION WORK SUPERVISOR

EXCAVATION WORK SUPERVISOR'S NAME

I, principal contractor/contractor name hereby appoint excavation work supervisor's name as the excavation work supervisor responsible for site address to supervise and carry out all the necessary inspections in terms of all excavation work.

You shall ensure that when becoming aware of any health and safety hazards in respect to excavation work that the necessary precautionary measures are taken and enforced.

You shall further ensure that the requirements of the Construction Regulations are at all times met. On identifying any shortfalls or hazards convey such information in writing to the construction supervisor.

This appointment is valid from date to the completion of the stipulated construction work.

....

Principal contractor's/contractor's full name Date

Kindly confirm your acceptance of this appointment by completing the following:

I, excavation work supervisor's full name understand the implications of the appointment as detailed above and confirm my acceptance.

....

Excavation work supervisor's full name Date

PLACE COMPANY LOGO

COMPANY NAME

COMPANY ADDRESS

OCCUPATIONAL HEALTH AND SAFETY ACT, ACT 85 OF 1993

CONSTRUCTION REGULATION 12 (1)

APPOINTMENT OF THE DEMOLITION WORK SUPERVISOR

DEMOLITION WORK SUPERVISOR'S NAME

I, principal contractor/contractor name hereby appoint demolition work supervisor's name as the demolition work supervisor responsible for site address to supervise and carry out all the necessary inspections in terms of all demolition work.

You shall ensure that when becoming aware of any health and safety hazards in respect to demolition work that the necessary precautionary measures are taken and enforced.

You shall further ensure that the requirements of the Construction Regulations are at all times met. On identifying any shortfalls or hazards convey such information in writing to the construction supervisor.

This appointment is valid from date to the completion of the stipulated construction work.

....

Principal contractor's/contractor's full name Date

Kindly confirm your acceptance of this appointment by completing the following:

I, demolition work supervisor's full name understand the implications of the appointment as detailed above and confirm my acceptance.

....

Demolition work supervisor's full name Date

PLACE COMPANY LOGO

COMPANY NAME

COMPANY ADDRESS

OCCUPATIONAL HEALTH AND SAFETY ACT, ACT 85 OF 1993

CONSTRUCTION REGULATION 14 (2)

APPOINTMENT OF THE SCAFFOLDING SUPERVISOR

SCAFFOLDING SUPERVISOR'S NAME

I, principal contractor/contractor name hereby appoint scaffolding supervisor's name as the scaffolding supervisor responsible for site address to supervise and carry out all the necessary inspections in terms of all scaffolding work.

You shall ensure that when becoming aware of any health and safety hazards in respect to scaffolding work that the necessary precautionary measures are taken and enforced.

You shall further ensure that the requirements of the Construction Regulations are at all times met. On identifying any shortfalls or hazards convey such information in writing to the construction supervisor.

This appointment is valid from date to the completion of the stipulated construction work.

....

Principal contractor's/contractor's full name Date

Kindly confirm your acceptance of this appointment by completing the following:

I, scaffolding supervisor's full name understand the implications of the appointment as detailed above and confirm my acceptance.

....

Scaffolding supervisor's full name Date

PLACE COMPANY LOGO

COMPANY NAME

COMPANY ADDRESS

OCCUPATIONAL HEALTH AND SAFETY ACT, ACT 85 OF 1993

CONSTRUCTION REGULATION 15 (1)

APPOINTMENT OF THE SUSPENDED PLATFORM SUPERVISOR

SUSPENDED PLATFORM SUPERVISOR'S NAME

I, principal contractor/contractor name hereby appoint suspended platform supervisor's name as the suspended platform supervisor responsible for site address to supervise and carry out all the necessary inspections in terms of all suspended platform work.

You shall ensure that when becoming aware of any health and safety hazards in respect to suspended platform work that the necessary precautionary measures are taken and enforced.

You shall further ensure that the requirements of the Construction Regulations are at all times met. On identifying any shortfalls or hazards convey such information in writing to the construction supervisor.

This appointment is valid from date to the completion of the stipulated construction work.

....

Principal contractor's/contractor's full name Date

Kindly confirm your acceptance of this appointment by completing the following:

I, suspended platform supervisor's full name understand the implications of the appointment as detailed above and confirm my acceptance.

....

Suspended platform supervisor's full name Date

PLACE COMPANY LOGO

COMPANY NAME

COMPANY ADDRESS

OCCUPATIONAL HEALTH AND SAFETY ACT, ACT 85 OF 1993

CONSTRUCTION REGULATION 17 (1)

APPOINTMENT OF THE MATERIAL HOIST INSPECTOR

MATERIAL HOIST INSPECTOR'S NAME

I, principal contractor/contractor name hereby appoint material hoist inspector's name as the material hoist inspector responsible for site address to supervise and carry out all the necessary inspections in terms of all material hoists on site.

You shall ensure that when becoming aware of any health and safety hazards in respect to material hoists that the necessary precautionary measures are taken and enforced.

You shall further ensure that the requirements of the Construction Regulations are at all times met. On identifying any shortfalls or hazards convey such information in writing to the construction supervisor.

This appointment is valid from date to the completion of the stipulated construction work.

....
Principal contractor's/contractor's full name Date

Kindly confirm your acceptance of this appointment by completing the following:

I, material hoist inspector's full name understand the implications of the appointment as detailed above and confirm my acceptance.

....
Material hoist inspector's full name Date

PLACE COMPANY LOGO

COMPANY NAME

COMPANY ADDRESS

OCCUPATIONAL HEALTH AND SAFETY ACT, ACT 85 OF 1993

CONSTRUCTION REGULATION 18 (1)

APPOINTMENT OF THE BATCH PLANT SUPERVISOR

BATCH PLANT SUPERVISOR'S NAME

I, principal contractor/contractor name hereby appoint batch plant supervisor's name as the batch plant supervisor responsible for site address to supervise and carry out all the necessary inspections in terms of all batch plants on site.

You shall ensure that when becoming aware of any health and safety hazards in respect to batch plants that the necessary precautionary measures are taken and enforced.

You shall further ensure that the requirements of the Construction Regulations are at all times met. On identifying any shortfalls or hazards convey such information in writing to the construction supervisor.

This appointment is valid from date to the completion of the stipulated construction work.

....

Principal contractor's/contractor's full name Date

Kindly confirm your acceptance of this appointment by completing the following:

I, batch plant supervisor's full name understand the implications of the appointment as detailed above and confirm my acceptance.

....

Batch plant supervisor's full name Date

PLACE COMPANY LOGO

COMPANY NAME

COMPANY ADDRESS

OCCUPATIONAL HEALTH AND SAFETY ACT, ACT 85 OF 1993

CONSTRUCTION REGULATION 19 (2) (g) (i)

APPOINTMENT OF THE EXPLOSIVE POWERED TOOLS ISSUER

EXPLOSIVE POWERED TOOLS ISSUER'S NAME

I, principal contractor/contractor name hereby appoint explosive powered tools issuer's name as the explosive powered tools issuer responsible for site address to issue, receive and record the issuing and receiving of all cartridges and nails or studs.

You shall ensure that when becoming aware of any health and safety hazards in respect to explosive powered tools that the necessary precautionary measures are taken and enforced.

You shall further ensure that the requirements of the Construction Regulations are at all times met. On identifying any shortfalls or hazards convey such information in writing to the construction supervisor.

This appointment is valid from date to the completion of the stipulated construction work.

....

Principal contractor's/contractor's full name Date

Kindly confirm your acceptance of this appointment by completing the following:

I, explosive powered tools issuer's full name understand the implications of the appointment as detailed above and confirm my acceptance.

....

Explosive powered tools issuer's full name Date

PLACE COMPANY LOGO

COMPANY NAME

COMPANY ADDRESS

OCCUPATIONAL HEALTH AND SAFETY ACT, ACT 85 OF 1993

CONSTRUCTION REGULATION 21 (1) (j)

APPOINTMENT OF THE CONSTRUCTION VEHICLES AND MOBILE PLANT INSPECTOR

CONSTRUCTION VEHICLES AND MOBILE PLANT INSPECTOR'S NAME

I, principal contractor/contractor name hereby appoint construction vehicles and mobile plant inspector's name as the construction vehicles and mobile plant inspector responsible for site address to inspect on a daily basis all construction vehicles and mobile plant.

You shall ensure that when becoming aware of any health and safety hazards in respect to construction vehicles and mobile plant that the necessary precautionary measures are taken and enforced.

You shall further ensure that the requirements of the Construction Regulations are at all times met. On identifying any shortfalls or hazards convey such information in writing to the construction supervisor.

This appointment is valid from date to the completion of the stipulated construction work.

....

Principal contractor's/contractor's full name Date

Kindly confirm your acceptance of this appointment by completing the following:

I, construction vehicles and mobile plant inspector's full name understand the implications of the appointment as detailed above and confirm my acceptance.

....

Construction vehicles and mobile plant inspector's full name Date

PLACE COMPANY LOGO

COMPANY NAME

COMPANY ADDRESS

OCCUPATIONAL HEALTH AND SAFETY ACT, ACT 85 OF 1993

CONSTRUCTION REGULATION 22 (e)

APPOINTMENT OF THE TEMPORARY ELECTRICAL INSTALLATION CONTROLLER

TEMPORARY ELECTRICAL INSTALLATION CONTROLLER'S NAME

I, principal contractor/contractor name hereby appoint temporary electrical installation controller's name as the temporary electrical installation controller responsible for site address to control all temporary electrical installations on site.

You shall ensure that when becoming aware of any health and safety hazards in respect to temporary electrical installations that the necessary precautionary measures are taken and enforced.

You shall further ensure that the requirements of the Construction Regulations are at all times met. On identifying any shortfalls or hazards convey such information in writing to the construction supervisor.

This appointment is valid from date to the completion of the stipulated construction work.

....

Principal contractor's/contractor's full name Date

Kindly confirm your acceptance of this appointment by completing the following:

I, temporary electrical installations controller's full name understand the implications of the appointment as detailed above and confirm my acceptance.

....

Temporary electrical installations controller's full name Date

PLACE COMPANY LOGO

COMPANY NAME

COMPANY ADDRESS

OCCUPATIONAL HEALTH AND SAFETY ACT, ACT 85 OF 1993

CONSTRUCTION REGULATION 26 (a)

APPOINTMENT OF THE STACKING AND STORAGE SUPERVISOR

STACKING AND STORAGE SUPERVISOR'S NAME

I, principal contractor/contractor name hereby appoint stacking and storage supervisor's name as the stacking and storage supervisor responsible for site address to manage all stacking and storage on site.

You shall ensure that when becoming aware of any health and safety hazards in respect to stacking and storage that the necessary precautionary measures are taken and enforced.

You shall further ensure that the requirements of the Construction Regulations are at all times met. On identifying any shortfalls or hazards convey such information in writing to the construction supervisor.

This appointment is valid from date to the completion of the stipulated construction work.

....

Principal contractor's/contractor's full name Date

Kindly confirm your acceptance of this appointment by completing the following:

I, stacking and storage supervisor's full name understand the implications of the appointment as detailed above and confirm my acceptance.

....

Stacking and storage supervisor's full name Date

PLACE COMPANY LOGO

COMPANY NAME

COMPANY ADDRESS

OCCUPATIONAL HEALTH AND SAFETY ACT, ACT 85 OF 1993

CONSTRUCTION REGULATION 27 (h)

APPOINTMENT OF THE FIRE EXTINGUISHER INSPECTOR

FIRE EXTINGUISHER INSPECTOR'S NAME

I, principal contractor/contractor name hereby appoint fire extinguisher inspector's name as the fire extinguishing inspector responsible for site address to carry out all inspections in respect to fire extinguishers.

You shall ensure that when becoming aware of any health and safety hazards in respect to fire extinguishers that the necessary precautionary measures are taken and enforced.

You shall further ensure that the requirements of the Construction Regulations are at all times met. On identifying any shortfalls or hazards convey such information in writing to the construction supervisor.

This appointment is valid from date to the completion of the stipulated construction work.

....

Principal contractor's/contractor's full name Date

Kindly confirm your acceptance of this appointment by completing the following:

I, fire extinguisher inspector's full name understand the implications of the appointment as detailed above and confirm my acceptance.

....

Fire extinguisher inspector's full name Date

ANNEXURE D

CHECKLISTS

COMPANY NAME/LOGO

SITE ADDRESS

Bricklaying Checklist for Contractors

QUESTION	EXPLANATION	COMMENT
1. Have you set aside enough space for deliveries of bricks?	Wherever space allows, have the pallets of bricks stored inside the site boundaries, making sure they do not block safe access and emergency exits. Locate pallets so the bricklayers' labourers can safely pick up the bricks below their shoulder height and safely move the bricks to where they are needed. If you are forced to store bricks on nature strips or other public space, make sure you comply with municipal Council requirements and properly barricade them to safeguard the public. Never block off footpaths in a way which forces people onto an un-barricaded public roadway.	
2. Are cement mixers being used safely?	Mixers should be well maintained and serviceable. Make sure they are fitted with proper guards around the pulley belts. Electrically powered mixers should have leads in good condition and should be protected by a residual current device (earth leakage). Petrol-driven mixers should be properly tuned and should never be used inside buildings unless there is very good natural ventilation to prevent deadly build up of carbon monoxide fumes. They should also not be used in cellars and basements.	
3. Have the bricklayers' scaffolds been properly constructed?	Scaffolds for bricklaying need to be built for heavy duty loads (up to 675 kg per platform per bay). They must be on firm foundations and built level and plumb. They need to be properly braced and rigidly tied to the building. They need proper temporary stairways or ladder access. Platforms should be at least 5 planks wide and fully decked with genuine scaffold planks in sound condition. All platforms over 2 metres need guardrails, midrails and toeboards. Brickguards are preferable. Trestle scaffolds should be heavy duty, fully planked, set up on firm horizontal surfaces and never used where a person or brick could fall more than 2 metres. Adjustable trestles need hardened steel locking pins -- not pieces of scrap reinforcing rod because a sudden impact on the trestle can shear them (just like bolt cutters can). Never "piggyback" trestles to gain extra height -- use the proper type of scaffold instead. Keep the scaffolds at least 4.6 metres away from live powerlines. If the potential fall height from the scaffold is more than 4 metres, it must be erected, altered and dismantled by a person with a WorkSafe certificate of competency appropriate to the type of scaffold.	

QUESTION	EXPLANATION	COMMENT
	Modular scaffolds should incorporate 2-plank platform brackets where practicable so that bricklayers can work from "split lifts" and lay the bricks above knee height and below shoulder height. Where platform brackets are set up between lifts and the fall distance from them is more than 2 metres, the lift immediately below the brackets should also be fully decked as a catch platform for falling debris, with an inside toeboard in addition to the outside guardrail, midrail and toeboard.	
4. Are the bricklayers using the scaffold safely?	Overloaded platforms can cause the scaffold to collapse. Heavy duty working platforms can be safely loaded up to 675 kg per bay. Typically, on one working platform bay, this might be something like allowance for up to two workers at any one time (160 kg), up to 100 bricks (around 400 kg), a drum of water (around 10 kg), a board of mortar (up to 80 kg) and some hand tools (around 5 kg). Clear access needs to be maintained along the full platform length. Broken bricks and debris should be regularly cleaned up from the platform and safely deposited off the scaffold. Bricklayers should not lay bricks above shoulder height because this greatly increases the risk of manual handling injuries. Get a new lift of scaffold put in at the right height so they don't have to over-reach.	
5. Are material hoists properly set up and used safely?	The person erecting and dismantling a material hoist must be competent, and the person who operates the hoist must also be competen. The hoist must be stable and vertical. It should be independently tied to the building – not just tied to the scaffold because if it overturns, it will pull the scaffold down with it. The hoist operator needs overhead protection. Use interlocked gates at scaffold platform landings. Make sure the hoist is well maintained and regularly inspected. Electrically powered hoists need residual current devices (earth leakage). Wheelbarrows should be placed on the hoist platform with the handles pointing towards the scaffold so the labourer can pick up the barrow without needing to step on to the elevated platform. Never allow or tolerate anyone riding on the platform – material hoists are not designed safely enough to support people.	
6. Is brick cleaning being done safely?	Brick cleaning involves the use of hydrochloric acid and water. Make sure hydrochloric acid containers are safely and securely stored when not in use. Make sure the workers understand the dangers of acid burns and know how to use acids safely. Make sure they are fully protected from acid splashes to the eyes and skin.	
NAME:	SIGNATURE:	DATE:

COMPANY NAME/LOGO

SCAFFOLD INSPECTION LIST

GSR 13.D

LOCATION OF SCAFFOLD	DATE IN SPECTED	APPOINTED COMPETENT PERSON'S NAME	APPOINTED COMPETENT PERSON'S SIGNATURE	CHECK CONDITION OF AND LIST IDENTIFIED SHORTFALLS AND CORRECTIVE ACTION				
				FRAMEWORK	PLATFORMS	TRESTLES	SUSPENDED SCAFFOLDS	RAMPS

ISSUES REQUIRING CHECKING

FRAMEWORK		PLATFORM	TRESTLES	SUSPENDED SCAFFOLD	RAMPS
Secure foundation Standards supported & secured Horizontally secured Vertically secured Catch nets where applicable	Fasteners Sole plates Ledgers secured Corrosion free	Sufficient Planks Toe-boards Condition of planks Guard rails fitted Safe access Free of waste	Platform Splaying of legs Framework	Platform Outriggers Suspension system Ropes	Framework Planks Angle of inclination Stepping laths Hand rails Toe-boards

COMPANY NAME/LOGO

SITE ADDRESS

Competent Person Scaffold Inspection Checklist

QUESTION	COMMENT
1. Are scaffolds and scaffold components inspected before each work shift by a competent person?	
2. Have employees who erect, disassemble, move, operate, repair, maintain, or inspect the scaffold been trained by a *competent person* to recognize the hazards associated with this type of scaffold and the performance of their duties related to this scaffold?	
3. Have employees who use the scaffold been trained by a qualified person to recognize the hazards associated it with this scaffold and know the performance of their duties relating to it?	
4. Is the maximum load capacity of this scaffold known and communicated to all employees?	
5. Is the load on the scaffold (including point loading) within the maximum load capacity of this particular scaffold?	
6. Is the scaffold plumb, square, and level?	
7. Is the scaffold on base plates and are mudsills level, sound, and rigid?	
8. Is there safe access to all scaffold platforms?	
9. Are all working platforms fully planked?	
10. Do planks extend at least 6 inches and no more than 12 inches over the supports?	
11. Are the planks in good condition and free of visible defects?	
12. Does the scaffold have all required guardrails and toeboards?	
13. Are 4:1 (height to width) scaffolds secured to a building or structure as required?	

NAME OF APPOINTED COMPETENT PERSON:	SIGNATURE:	DATE:

COMPANY NAME/LOGO

SITE ADDRESS

Competent Person Scaffold Inspection Checklist

QUESTION	EXPLANATION	COMMENT
1. Have you allowed for your scaffolding costs in your contract price?	If you quote the job without considering the types of scaffolds and the quantities of scaffolding equipment you need to do the work safely and legally, you could lose big money when you provide the necessary scaffolding.	
2. Are your scaffolders properly competent?	You must make certain that anyone constructing, or directly supervising the workers constructing any scaffold from which a person or materials could fall ensure that the scaffold erectors are competent.	
3. Is the scaffold strong enough for the loads?	Bricklayers, stonemasons, concretors and demolition workers need heavy duty scaffolds which can safely support up to 675 kg per platform per bay. Carpenters and general trades may need at least medium duty scaffolds which can safely support up to 450 kg per platform per bay. Light duty scaffolds are limited to 225 kg per platform per bay. In estimating loads on scaffold platforms, a person is assumed to weigh 80 kg. Check the supplier's information for the type of scaffolding systems you are using	
4. Is the scaffold stable?	Scaffolds can collapse if they are built on soft ground without timber soleplates to properly distribute the load, if they are too close to trenches or excavations, if they are not properly braced and tied to the supporting structure, or if they are badly out of level.	
5. Does the scaffold protect the workers and other people?	Planks should be genuine scaffold planks in good condition, of uniform thickness (to prevent trip hazards) and secured against uplift. Platforms should be fully decked across their full width and free of gaps. All platforms higher than 2 metres should have guardrails, midrails and toeboards (or brickguards) fixed to each open side and end. Where debris from the work can cause danger, it may be necessary to sheet the scaffold in shadecloth. Never use hessian because it can very easily catch fire.	
6. Is there safe access to every scaffold platform?	Properly constructed temporary stairways or ladder access is needed to all working platforms. Climbing up and down the scaffold framework is very dangerous. Ladders should be securely fixed to prevent movement, pitched at a gradient not less than 1 in 4 nor more than 1 in 6, and they should extend at least 900 mm above the platform so they can be safely climbed.	
7. Are scaffolds a safe distance from powerlines?	No part of a metal scaffold should be closer than 4 metres from any live powerlines.	

QUESTION	EXPLANATION	COMMENT
8. Are your scaffolders working safely?	While it is under construction, the scaffold should be isolated from other workers and the general public. Scaffolders' tools should be stowed in holders on their scaffold belt. Scaffolders should work from a full deck of planks whenever possible. They should fix a guard-rail for their own protection as they go, leaving it in place until that part of the scaffold is dismantled. Scaffolders working underneath should wear safety helmets. On large jobs, they should have the scaffolding equipment crane lifted, or they should use a winch or gin wheel to reduce manual handling risks.	
9. Are your scaffold users working safely?	Workers must use the scaffold safely. They must not overload the platforms or store material in a dangerous way where it could be knocked off the scaffold. Clear access should be maintained along the full length of platforms. They should not climb on guardrails to get extra height. They should not make the scaffold unsafe by removing planks, ties or guardrails.	
10. Are your scaffolds being regularly inspected?	You must not allow work to start from a scaffold until the construction of the scaffold is complete. Get the scaffolder in charge of the work to fill in a handover certificate and keep it on site until the scaffold has been dismantled. Make sure a certificated scaffolder or other competent person inspects all alterations or additions to the scaffold. Have a thorough inspection done at least every month and keep a copy of the inspection record on site. Get any necessary repairs to the scaffold done before it is put back into use.	
NAME OF APPOINTED COMPETENT PERSON:	SIGNATURE:	DATE:

COMPANY NAME/LOGO

SITE ADDRESS

Dangerous Goods Checklist for Contractors

QUESTION	EXPLANATION	COMMENT
1. Are Dangerous Goods used?	Dangerous Goods used at the site may include explosives, flammable liquids such as petrol, kerosene, turps and flammable paints; corrosives such as hydrochloric acid; oxy/acetylene welding sets and LPG. Make sure there is a Material Safety Data Sheet for each Dangerous Good. Get these from the supplier or manufacturer of the substance. Provide correct personal protective equipment for chemical use. Ensure first aid provisions are suitable for Dangerous Goods on the site, including adequate eye wash. Make sure workers have been trained in the use of Dangerous Goods.	
2. Are flammable and combustible liquids used at the site?	Store flammable liquids away from any ignition sources or sources of heat. Keep containers closed when not in use and secured when the site is unattended. Remove all combustible materials from areas where flammable liquids are stored, used or decanted. Transfer flammable liquids in a safe manner where a dry chemical fire extinguisher is available. Ensure nobody smokes near flammable or combustible substances and display NO SMOKING signs where these are stored. Oily rags can spontaneously combust in hot weather and should not be left in piles.	
3. Is LPG used at the site?	Keep LPG cylinders in an upright position at all times. Restrain them from falling and protect them from vehicle damage. Keep cylinder valves closed when not in use. Ensure LPG is not used near ignition sources or while smoking. Provide a dry chemical fire extinguisher. LPG cylinders are never to be turned upside down to freeze pipes. Ensure appliances are compatible and a regulator is to be used where necessary. Store cylinders in a well ventilated area away from combustible materials. Provide security for cylinders when the site is unattended.	
4. Are welding sets used at the site?	Ensure attached equipment is compatible and a regulator set is provided where necessary. Provide a flashback arrester. Keep cylinders upright and protected from impact. Provide personal protective equipment for welding.	
5. Are explosives used at the site?	Keep explosives in a locked receptacle. Do not leave discarded detonator boxes on the site. Do not leave excess explosives on an unattended site. You need to comply with the Explosives Regulations in rspect to permission that must be obtained.	
NAME	SIGNATURE:	DATE:

COMPANY NAME/LOGO

SITE ADDRESS

Demolition Checklist for Contractors

QUESTION	EXPLANATION	COMMENT
1. Has the building been checked for asbestos?	If the building or plant contains asbestos, get aN - approved asbestos removal contractor to remove and properly dispose of all asbestos-containing material. Where possible, have all asbestos removal work completed before starting the rest of the demolition.	
2. Have all services been identified?	Make sure you have located all electric power lines and cables, gas lines, telecommunication lines and water and sewerage lines. Look for septic tanks and underground storage tanks and check their condition. Don't simply rely on the original site plans and drawings. Get expert help from the supply and distribution authorities.	
3. Has power and gas been disconnected?	Confirm that power and gas has been properly disconnected by the distribution authorities. After this, test outlets to double check that all power and gas has been stopped. Safely flush gas out of disconnected lines and storages.	
4. Are fire services available?	Keep existing lines and hoses in place for as long as possible. Provide adequate temporary fire services where necessary. Get advice from your local fire brigade.	
5. Has the demolition sequence been planned?	The sequence in which a building is demolished can be critical to the safety of the workers and the general public. Whenever you are in doubt, or whenever you are dealing with unusual structures or structures incorporating pre-stressed concrete reinforced members, get expert advice from an experienced structural engineer.	
6. Are demolition tools and equipment being used safely?	Check that compressors, jackhammers and other pneumatic tools are properly maintained and fully serviceable. Make sure all air-hose connections are secured with safety pins to prevent dangerous blowouts. Do not use petrol or diesel driven compressors or equipment in cellars or any badly ventilated areas. Check that concrete cutting equipment is the right sort for the tasks. Check that oxy cutting equipment is in good condition, properly secured and close to fire extinguishers. Make sure workers are using the right personal protective equipment for the tools, such as ear muffs, breathing masks, protective glasses, head shields, gloves, or rawhide boilermaker's jackets to prevent burns	

QUESTION	EXPLANATION	COMMENT
7. Are workers protected from falls?	Properly cover or securely barricade all floor or roof penetrations, lift shaft entrances and doorways where staircases are to be removed. Provide properly constructed heavy duty scaffolds. Never allow demolition workers to work unprotected at heights. Where safety harnesses are necessary, make sure they are serviceable, properly worn and securely fixed to anchorages with a safe load capacity of at least 1.5 ton. Make sure inertia reel lines cannot be severed on sharp edges.	
8. Is the public properly protected?	Buildings adjacent or close to public space should have a full-height heavy duty perimeter scaffold to safely contain any debris. It may need to be sheeted in chain mesh, or shade cloth, or both. Never use hessian because it easily catches fire. Where demolition work is being carried out from the scaffold, fix ply sheets from the working platform to the guardrail. Laying old carpet over the platforms and guardrails will help to contain debris on the platform. Where necessary, provide properly designed and constructed overhead protective gantries or covered ways over footpaths and laneways. Make sure you comply with all requirements of the local municipal Council.	
9. Are suspended floors safe for the loads?	Get a structural engineer to determine the loading capacity of floors before placing earthmoving equipment, heavy plant or building rubble on them. Floor capacity may need to be increased by back-propping the floors with shoring frames or rigidly connected systems of adjustable building props. Regularly monitor floor loads and rubble build-up to safeguard from overloading.	
NAME APPOINTED COMPETENT PERSON:	SIGNATURE:	DATE:

COMPANY NAME/LOGO

SITE ADDRESS

Earth Leakage Control Inspection Checklist for Contractors

1. Has the earth leakage protection unit been fitted?		
2. Does unit operate correctly when test button is pressed?		
3. Are all units labelled?		
4. Are all sockets protected by earth leakage?		
5. Are all sockets numbered correctly?		
6. Are all units in generally good condition/		
7. Have all sockets been tested?		
8. Have all portable units been inspected and tested?		
9. Has mA been recorded?		
10. Is the standard 16mA to 30 mA replacement used		

REPLACEMENT CRITERIA

The earth leakage unit must be replaced if the reading exceeds 30 milli amps or if it is below 15 milli amps

Location	DB No	EL Setting	Circuit	Switch Socket No	MA Reading

REMARKS/RECOMMENDATIONS:		
NAME OF COMPETENT PERSON:	SIGNATURE OF COMPETENT PERSON:	DATE

COMPANY NAME/LOGO

SITE ADDRESS

Electrical Hazards Checklist for Contractors

QUESTION	EXPLANATION	COMMENT
1. Are switchboards properly constructed and set up?	Ensure supply switchboards are of robust design and build. They should have: • a tie bar to prevent strain at termination of cables/wiring insulated stands for the support of cables and extension leads • a lockable door that cannot damage leads • a way of keeping the door open for electrical installation work • weatherproofing where outdoors or located anywhere subject to water • a clear area of 1 m at the front • a lockable cover over circuit breakers but not over main switches/isolating switches. Where a meter panel and fuse assembly is fitted, make sure switchboards have an endorsed locking device.	
2. Are all circuits, portable equipment, electrical plant and tools protected from earth leakage?	Check that every final sub circuit, all portable electrical equipment, electrical plant and tools are protected.	
3. Are the right general purpose outlets being used?	Check that general purpose outlets with double pole switches are used for 240 volt sockets on portable equipment.	
4. Are portable outlet devices suitable?	Double adapters are not suitable for normal use on construction sites. Check that multi-plug portable outlet devices comply with SABS 0142.	
5. Is cabling protected from mechanical damage?	Make sure cabling has protection where there is a risk of mechanical damage. If a change occurs that introduces a risk, provide protection. Also ensure that there is no unauthorised work on portable buildings, such as drilling, nailing, screwing and fixing of attachments.	
6. Are electrically powered tools and flexible leads in a safe condition?	One way to make sure tools and leads are likely to be safe is by having them inspected, tested and tagged by a electrician when they are first brought on site and then at regular intervals. Keep a site register of inspections. Make sure unserviceable tools or leads are immediately withdrawn from service until they are repaired or replaced.	

QUESTION	EXPLANATION	COMMENT
7. Have Electrical Certificates of Compliance been issued?	Ensure that electrical Certificates of Compliance have been issued for all construction wiring, including switchboards, before use	
8. Have earth leakages been tested?	Ensure that earth leakages are tested by operation of the test button before each use, and tested for tripping current and time by a electrician every calendar month while used on site.	
9. Are portable generators suitable?	Check that portable generators are: • fully serviceable and properly maintained • fitted with a 30 mA eartjh leakage • where supplying a fixed installation, installed by a registered electrical contractor, a Electrical Certificate of compliance is provided and, before use, generators are inspected by an electrician • where supplying portable tools and equipment, provided with earth and bonding connections according to the manufacturer/supplier information displayed on the generator.	
10. Are leads set out safely?	Check that leads are not lying in mud or water or in areas where they can be damaged or become tripping hazards. Use stable, insulated lead stands to keep them above head-height. Do not allow leads to be wrapped around scaffolds or formwork – use S-shaped off-cuts of steel reinforcing bar sheathed in cut-off lengths of garden hose instead.	
11. Are plant and temporary structures a safe distance from powerlines?	Make sure there is always a safe distance between live powerlines and cranes, earth moving equipment, elevating work platforms, hoists, scaffolds, formwork and portable ladders by observing "no go zone" safe clearances.	
12. Is electrical installation and repair work being done safely?	Make sure that all electrical installation and repair work is supervised by licensed electricians	
NAME OF APPOINTED ELECTRICAL CONTROLLER:	SIGNATURE OF APPOINTED ELECTRICAL CONTROLLER:	DATE:

COMPANY NAME/LOGO

SITE ADDRESS

ELECTRICAL INSTALLATIONS CHECKLIST

DISTRIBUTION BOARDS AND EARTH LEAKAGE				
		COMMENTS	YES	NO
1	Are distribution boards numbered?			
2	Has earth leakage being installed?			
3	Is the earth leakage operational when tested?			
4	Is the main circuit breaker readily identifiable and accessible at all times?			
5	Are all openings covered to ensure that there are no bare conductors exposed?			
6	Are the symbolic signs clearly displayed and understandable?			
7	Are distribution boards colour coded (orange)?			
8	Are all the distribution boards face plates securely fastened and in place?			
9	Are all switches clearly labeled?			
THE GENERAL ELECTRICAL INSTALLATION				
1	Is all wiring securely fastened and not hanging loose?			
2	Are there any bare conductors/wiring?			
3	Is all labeling correct and in place/			
4	Is there any heat or moisture present that could result in a hazardous situation?			
5	In those instances where there are bare conductors required for the process is the necessary signage in place?			
6	Are all earth leakage straps in place?			
7	Has all the earth leakage been tested?			
8	Has all electrical equipment been externally inspected and found in good condition?			
9	Has a lockout facility been fitted to all electrical equipment?			
10	Has a polarity test been conducted?			
11	Are all electrical switched and plugs in a good and safe condition?			
12	Are all distribution boards kept clear?			
RECOMMENDATIONS:				
SIGNATURE OF INSPECTOR:		DATE OF INSPECTION:		

COMPANY NAME/LOGO

SITE ADDRESS

Ergonomics Checklist for Contractors

Materials Handling

What heavy materials or equipment are being handled on site – drywall, rebar, concrete forms, anything over 20 pounds?

QUESTION	YES	NO	COMMENT
Do any workers have to lift more than 20 KG at one time without help?			
Do workers have to lift more than 10 KG often? **If yes**, how can this be changed?			
Are there handles to help carry materials?			
If yes, are the handles easy to use and comfortable?			
Are workers told to get someone's help to lift heavy materials?			
Are there carts, dollies, or other aids readily available for moving materials?			
If yes, are the carts being used?			
If no, why not?			
If no, is the site clear enough to permit the use of carts?			
Are materials delivered as close as possible to where they will be used?			
If no, how can this be changed?			
On what jobs do workers have to lift overhead?			
How can this lifting be avoided?			
Are materials stored at floor or ground level?			
If yes, do workers have to bend down to lift materials?			
Can the materials be stored at waist height?			
On which tasks do workers have to stretch to pick up or lift materials?			
Can the materials be kept closer?			

Tools			
QUESTION	YES	NO	COMMENT
Are tools sharp and in good condition?			
Which tools are very heavy or not well balanced?			
Which tools vibrate too much?			
Which tools must be used while in a difficult position?			
Which tools have poor handle design? • grips too big or too small? handles that are too short and dig into hands? • handles with ridges that dig into hands? • slippery handles?			
Which tools require bending of wrists to use?			
Do gloves ever make it hard to grip tools?			
Are there other tools with a better design?			
If yes, what are they?			
Repetitive Work			
Which tasks or jobs use the same motion dozens of times an hour for more than 1 hour per day?			
What are the motions?			
Can the number of repetitions be reduced by job rotation or rest breaks?			
Awkward Postures			
Which tasks or jobs involve work above the shoulder more than 1 hour per day?			
Can scaffolds, platforms, or other equipment cut down on the need to work overhead?			
Are knee pads or cushions available and are they used?			
Can equipment be used to reduce kneeling?			
Which jobs require workers to stay in one position for a long time?			

D. CHECKLISTS

QUESTION	YES	NO	COMMENT
Can rotation or rest breaks be used to reduce time in awkward postures?			
Which jobs require a lot of twisting or turning?			
Which jobs require a lot of bending?			
How can the need to twist or bend be reduced?			
Standing			
What jobs require workers to stand all day, especially on concrete floors?			
Can anti-fatigue matting be used?			
Is it possible to use adjustable stools to allow workers to rest periodically?			
Surfaces for Walking and Working			
Are working and walking surfaces clean and dry?			
Are the surfaces unobstructed?			
Are the surfaces even?			
Seating			
What jobs require sitting all day?			
Are the seats well-designed, easy to adjust and comfortable?			
In heavy equipment, do workers have to lean forward to see/do their work?			
Does the seating in any heavy equipment vibrate a lot?			
Weather			
Do workers have enough protection from heat, cold, rain, wind, and sun?			
Lighting			
Are work areas well lit to prevent tripping and falling?			
Is there enough light to do the work?			
Are there areas where glare is a problem?			

Production pressures			
QUESTION	YES	NO	COMMENT
Do any workers work piece rate?			
Have supervisors or workers been under production pressures that could lead to shortcuts and injuries?			
How could this problem be reduced? More rest breaks?_____ More safety meetings?_____ A special safety rep on site?_____ Other_____			
Training			
What training have workers had on ergonomics preventing musculoskeletal disorders?			
What training have supervisors had on ergonomics preventing musculoskeletal disorders?			
Musculoskeletal Symptoms			
Do workers feel free to report symptoms?			
Have any workers been reporting muscle pain, tingling, numbness, loss of strength, or loss of joint movement?			
If yes, where? Back_____ Neck_____ Shoulder_____ Arm_____ Wrist_____ Knee_____			
Which trades have the most problems?			
And what may be the main cause(s)? Repetitive motion_____ Awkward postures________ Fixed postures _____ Heavy lifting_____ Not enough rest breaks _____ Other_____			
Do workers often appear exhausted at the end of the day?			

Solutions			
QUESTION	YES	NO	COMMENT
What jobs on site are the most hazardous for musculoskeletal injuries?			
Most hazardous jobs for musculoskeletal injuries			
What has been done to get worker ideas to help reduce musculoskeletal injuries on the job?			
What can be done working together to reduce these injuries?			
What can be done to reduce the hazards or make the jobs easier?			

Proposed solutions		
Most Effective	**Easiest to Implement**	**Least Expensive**
Least Effective	**Hardest to Implement**	**Most Expensive**
1. 2. 3. 4.		

COMPANY NAME/LOGO

SITE ADDRESS

First Aid Box and Equipment Checklist for Contractors

QUESTION	YES	NO
1. Wound cleaner/antiseptic (100ml)		
2. Swabs for cleaning wounds		
3. Cotton wool for padding (100 g)		
4. Sterile gauze (minimum quantity 10)		
5. 1 Pair of forceps (for splinters)		
6. 1 Pair scissors (minimum size 100 mm)		
7. Set of safety pins		
8. 4 Triangular bandages		
9. Four roller bandages (75 mm x 5 m)		
10. Four roller bandages (100 mm x 5 m)		
11. One roll elastic adhesive bandage (25 mm x 3m)		
12. 1 Non-allergic adhesive strip (25 mm x3 m)		
13. 1 Packet of adhesive dressing strips (minimum quantity, 10 assorted sizes)		
14. 4 First aid dressings (150 mm x 100 mm)		
15. 4 First aid dressings (75 mm x 100 mm)		
16. 2 Straight splints		
17. Disposable latex gloves (2 pairs medium and 2 pairs large)		
18. 2 CPR mouth pieces or similar devices		
GENERAL FINDINGS		
1. Box completely stocked ac cording to minimum requirements		
2. Name of first aider on box		
3. Box clearly indicated by use of symbolic signs		
4. "ISSUE BOOK" contained in box		
5. Qualified First-aider available when needed		
6. Box removable in an emergency		
7. Box in generally good condition		

NAME:	SIGNATURE:	DATE:

COMPANY NAME/LOGO

SITE ADDRESS

Formwork & Concreting Checklist For Contractors

QUESTION	EXPLANATION	COMMENT
1. Has the formwork system been properly designed?	Use an experienced structural engineer to design the formwork system for suspended concrete floors and beams. Keep a copy of the design drawings and loading calculations on site. Make sure you know how long the concrete must cure before the formwork can be dismantled.	
2. Has the formwork been properly constructed?	Formwork components (such as shoring frames and braces, heavy duty modular or frame-type scaffolding members, tri-shores, adjustable props, adjustable base plates, sole plates, scaffold tubes and couplers, U-heads and bearers) need to be in a serviceable condition. Check that the formwork is on firm foundations and has been constructed in accordance with the design plan. Make sure the formwork equipment is the sort and capacity specified in the design plan. Make sure adjustable building props are tied to each other or to the shoring frames so they cannot collapse when released.	
3. Is the formwork being laid safely?	The method used to lay out and secure the form ply must safeguard the formworkers from falling. When they need to work from the formwork itself, make sure they have a full deck of scaffold planks and safe access. When laying additional sheets from the formwork deck, workers should stay clear of the leading edge, pushing out the sheets as they go. Perimeter edge protection (temporary guardrailing or scaffolding) needs to be provided. Make sure the formworkers have safe and secure access to the form deck area.	
4. Is steel fixing being done safely?	Make sure plastic protective caps are always placed on the ends of starter bars to safeguard workers. When fixing steel for concrete walls and columns, steel fixers will need properly constructed scaffolds. Steel fixers need protective glasses when using bolt cutters to stop steel fragments from wounding their eyes.	
5. Are wall and column shutters safely lifted and properly secured?	Formwork shutters need to be securely slung and controlled with a tagline when they are being crane-lifted. Do not allow large shutters to be lifted in strong winds. Wherever possible, push-pull angled props should be fixed to cast-in slab anchors. Avoid using friction anchors. Formworkers fixing she-bolts need properly constructed scaffolds to work from.	

QUESTION	EXPLANATION	COMMENT
6. Are concrete pumps being used safely?	Concrete pumps must be well maintained and fully serviceable. Boom-type units must be operated by a person who is competent Make sure boom-type units are correctly set up with fully extended outriggers and are at least 6 metres clear of any electricity transmission lines or at least 3 metres clear of any electricity distribution lines. Pump lines need to be cleaned out after each use.	
7. Are concrete vibrators being used safely?	Check that vibrators are well maintained and fully serviceable. Electrically powered types should be protected with earthleakage. Do not use petrol-driven vibrators in cellars or other poorly ventilated areas.	
8. Are the concretors working safely?	Make sure there are no open sides or penetrations where a worker could fall more than 2 metres. Where necessary, provide temporary guardrailing or a heavy duty perimeter scaffold.	
9. Is formwork being stripped safely?	When stripping the underside of a suspended floor slab, barricade the area from other workers. Make sure people doing the stripping are working from properly constructed scaffolds or properly planked shoring frames. Never allow "drop stripping" of form ply and formwork.	
NAME OF APPOINTED COMPETENT PERSON:	SIGNATURE:	DATE:

COMPANY NAME/LOGO

SITE ADDRESS

Hand Tools and Equipment Checklist for Contractors

QUESTION	YES	NO	COMMENT
Are all tools and equipment (both company and employee owned) used by employees at their workplace in good condition?			
Are hand tools such as chisels and punches, which develop mushroomed heads during use, reconditioned or replaced as necessary?			
Are broken or fractured handles on hammers, axes and similar equipment replaced promptly?			
Are worn or bent wrenches replaced regularly?			
Are appropriate handles used on files and similar tools?			
Are employees made aware of the hazards caused by faulty or improperly used hand tools?			
Are appropriate safety glasses, face shields, etc. used while using hand tools or equipment which might produce flying materials or be subject to breakage?			
Are jacks checked periodically to ensure they are in good operating condition?			
Are tool handles wedged tightly in the head of all tools?			
Are tool cutting edges kept sharp so the tool will move smoothly without binding or skipping?			
Are tools stored in dry, secure locations where they won't be tampered with?			
Is eye and face protection used when driving hardened or tempered spuds or nails?			
NAME:	SIGNATURE:		DATE:

COMPANY NAME/LOGO

SITE ADDRESS

Hazardous Substances Checklist for Contractors

QUESTION	EXPLANATION	COMMENT
1. Are Hazardous Substances used at the site?	A hazardous substance can be identified by a warning such as "POISON", "DANGEROUS POISON" or "HAZARDOUS" on the label. Hazardous substances may include timber treatments, pesticides, fungicides, hydrochloric acid, glues, paints and thinners. Hazardous substances can also be Dangerous Goods.	
2. Have you provided information and training?	Provide Material Safety Data Sheets on all Hazardous Substances. Get these from the supplier or manufacturer. Check all containers are labelled when purchasing Hazardous substances and ensure that the label remains intact and is readable. Instruct and train workers on the safe use of substances.	
3. Have you conducted a risk assessment?	Determine if there is potential for harm associated with the use of the hazardous substance. Refer to the label and Material Safety Data Sheet. Reduce the risk by using a less toxic product, provide ventilation, reduce the number of people exposed and ensure worker use personal protective equipment and clothing.	
4. Are records kept?	Keep a register of Hazardous Substances and Material Safety Data Sheets. Record results of risk assess-ments.	
NAME:	SIGNATURE:	DATE:

COMPANY NAME/LOGO

SITE ADDRESS

Housekeeping Checklist for Contractors

WALKING-WORKING SURFACES General Work Environment			
QUESTION	YES	NO	COMMENT
Is a documented, functioning housekeeping program in place?			
Are all worksites clean, sanitary, and orderly?			
Are work surfaces kept dry or is appropriate means taken to assure the surfaces are slip-resistant?			
Are all spilled hazardous materials or liquids, including blood and other potentially infectious materials, cleaned up immediately and according to proper procedures?			
Is combustible scrap, debris and waste stored safely and removed from the worksite properly?			
Are accumulations of combustible dust routinely removed from elevated surfaces including the overhead structure of buildings, etc.?			
Is combustible dust cleaned up with a vacuum system to prevent the dust from going into suspension?			
Is metallic or conductive dust prevented from entering or accumulating on or around electrical enclosures or equipment?			
Are covered metal waste cans used for oily and paint-soaked waste?			
Walkways			
Are aisles and passageways kept clear?			
Are aisles and walkways marked as appropriate?			
Are wet surfaces covered with non-slip materials?			
Are holes in the floor, sidewalk or other walking surface repaired properly, covered or otherwise made safe?			
Is there safe clearance for walking in aisles where motorized or mechanical handling equipment is operating?			

QUESTION	YES	NO	COMMENT
Are materials or equipment stored in such a way that sharp projectives will not interfere with the walkway?			
Are spilled materials cleaned up immediately?			
Are changes of direction or elevation readily identifiable?			
Are aisles or walkways that pass near moving or operating machinery, welding operations or similar operations arranged so employees will not be subjected to potential hazards?			
Is adequate headroom provided for the entire length of any aisle or walkway?			
Are standard guardrails provided wherever aisle or walkway surfaces are elevated more than 30 inches above any adjacent floor or the ground?			
Are bridges provided over conveyors and similar hazards?			
Floor and Wall Openings			
Are floor openings guarded by a cover, a guardrail, or equivalent on all sides (except at entrance to stairways or ladders)?			
Are toeboards installed around the edges of permanent floor openings (where persons may pass below the opening)?			
Are skylight screens of such construction and mounting that they will withstand a load of at least 200 pounds?			
Is the glass in the windows, doors, glass walls, etc., which are subject to human impact, of sufficient thickness and type for the condition of use?			
Are grates or similar type covers over floor openings such as floor drains of such design that foot traffic or rolling equipment will not be affected by the grate spacing?			
Are unused portions of service pits and pits not actually in use either covered or protected by guardrails or equivalent?			
Are manhole covers, trench covers and similar covers, plus their supports designed to carry a truck rear axle load of at least 20,000 pounds when located in roadways and subject to vehicle traffic?			

QUESTION	YES	NO	COMMENT
Are floor or wall openings in fire resistive construction provided with doors or covers compatible with the fire rating of the structure and provided with a self-closing feature when appropriate?			
Stairs and Stairways			
Are standard stair rails or handrails on all stairways having four or more risers?			
Are all stairways at least 22 inches wide?			
Do stairs have landing platforms not less than 30 inches in the direction of travel and extend 22 inches in width at every 12 feet or less of vertical rise?			
Do stairs angle no more than 50 and no less than 30 degrees?			
Are step risers on stairs uniform from top to bottom?			
Are steps on stairs and stairways designed or provided with a surface that renders them slip resistant?			
Are stairway handrails located between 30 and 34 inches above the leading edge of stair treads?			
Do stairway handrails have at least 3 inches of clearance between the handrails and the wall or surface they are mounted on?			
Where doors or gates open directly on a stairway, is there a platform provided so the swing of the door does not reduce the width of the platform to less than 21 inches?			
Where stairs or stairways exit directly into any area where vehicles may be operated, are adequate barriers and warnings provided to prevent employees stepping into the path of traffic?			
Do stairway landings have a dimension measured in the direction of travel, at least equal to the width of the stairway?			
Elevated Surfaces			
Are signs posted, when appropriate, showing the elevated surface load capacity?			
Are surfaces elevated more than 30 inches above the floor or ground provided with standard guardrails?			

QUESTION	YES	NO	COMMENT
Are all elevated surfaces (beneath which people or machinery could be exposed to falling objects) provided with standard 4-inch toeboards?			
Is a permanent means of access and egress provided to elevated storage and work surfaces?			
Is required headroom provided where necessary?			
Is material on elevated surfaces piled, stacked or racked in a manner to prevent it from tipping, falling, collapsing, rolling or spreading?			
Are dock boards or bridge plates used when transferring materials between docks and trucks or rail cars?			

NAME:	SIGNATURE:	DATE:

COMPANY NAME/LOGO

LADDER INSPECTION CHECKLIST

GSR 13.A.(1)

ITEM	INSPECTION CRITERIA	COMMENT
	PORTABLE LADDERS	
1	LADDER NUMBERED	
2	ALL RUNGS FIRM DO NOT MOVE BY HAND	
3	NO CRACKS OR BENDS	
4	NO LOOSE NAILS, SCREWS ETC	
5	LADDER STABLE (CHECK HINGES FIRM & STOPS ON SPREADERS)	
6	LADDER CASTORS (WHEELS), BRAKES AND PLATFORM IN GOOD CONDITION	
7	CHECK EXTENSION SYSTEM	
8	CHECK EXTENSION LOCKS FOR SAFETY	
9	NON – SLIP DEVICES IN GOOD CONDITION	
10	NO PAINT ON WOODEN LADDERS	
	FIXED LADDERS	
11	LADDER NUMBERED	
12	NO DAMAGE OR MISSING RUNGS	
13	CAGE 700MM AWAY FROM LEVEL OF RUNGS	
14	ALL METAL PARTS IN GOOD CONDITION (CRACKS)	

APPOINTED COMPETENT INSPECTOR'S NAME:	SITE ADDRESS:	
APPOINTED COMPETENT INSPECTOR'S SIGNATURE:	DATE:	LADDER ID NO:

COMPANY NAME/LOGO

SITE ADDRESS

Personal Protection Checklist for Contractors

QUESTION	EXPLANATION	COMMENT
1. Have you identified your workers' personal protection needs?	Have a good look at the various types of work, the plant, equipment and chemicals used and the locations where work takes place. Any source of danger to workers' health or safety needs to be eliminated altogether or, where this is not practicable, the risks must be properly controlled. The best and most fool-proof ways to control risk is to isolate the source of danger from people or to use physical or presence-sensing guarding to prevent people coming into contact with the danger. But where this can not be done, or when it does not fully control the risk, use properly understood safe work procedures and the right combination of personal protective equipment (PPE) to fully safeguard workers.	
2. Have you posted the necessary personal protection signs?	To be on the safe side, you should declare the entire site a safety helmet and protective footwear area, and post the safety signs for these prominently at site entrances. Signpost any particular areas where workers will need hearing protection, safety glasses, gloves or breathing masks. Post signs and notices in amenities sheds to remind workers of what types of PPE are needed for various types of work.	
3. Have you made sure the right PPE has been provided?	If you are using PPE as a way of controlling risks, it is your responsibility to supply your workers with the right equipment. Insist that your supplier provides equipment complying with the appropriate Australian Standards and all necessary information on the correct fitting, cleaning and maintenance of the equipment. So far as possible, allow your workers to select the particular model so that it gives them maximum personal comfort. Comfortable PPE gets worn, while "one size fits all" PPE which is uncomfortable is only worn under sufferance.	
4. Do your workers understand why they need PPE?	Take the time and effort to make sure your workers know what the possible consequences to their health and safety may be if they do not use the right PPE. If they properly understand what can go wrong, they are more likely to use PPE without being constantly told. If workers are reluctant to use PPE, encourage them to help you develop a better way to do the work so that they won't need PPE.	
5. Are workers trained in the use of PPE?	Some types of PPE have particular, fitting, testing, cleaning and inspecting requirements. Where this is the case, make sure workers have been properly instructed in these procedures and can demonstrate them correctly.	

QUESTION	EXPLANATION	COMMENT
6. Is PPE use being adequately monitored?	PPE is only as good as the degree to which it is properly used. Providing a worker with PPE and then failing to make sure it is being used is simply not good enough. Conduct regular checks. Insist that the rules for PPE are always followed. Take appropriate action to make this stick.	
7. Is PPE being inspected and replaced as necessary?	Faulty PPE is sometimes worse than no PPE because it can give the worker a false sense of security. For example, the use of incompatible components in safety harness systems can cause the "roll out" of snap hooks which may result in a worker falling to their death. Make sure PPE is checked regularly for serviceability and compatibility.	
8. Do you review your PPE needs?	New products come on to the market which may provide you with a way of controlling risks without the need for PPE any longer. For example, recent innovations in temporary guardrailing systems now mean there is a product to suit most types of roofing work, reducing the need to rely on safety harness systems. Also, new and improved PPE products are regularly being introduced. Keep up to date through trade magazines, your safety equipment supplier and your industry association.	
NAME:	SIGNATURE:	DATE:

COMPANY NAME/LOGO

SITE ADDRESS

Portable Electrical Tools, Lights, and Appliances Register

ITEM	INSPECTOR SIGNATURE	DEFECTS	REPORTED TO	DATE	RECTIFICATION TARGET DATE	ARTISAN SIGNATURE
1. Guards in good condition						
2. Connections tight						
3. No cable joints						
4. Isolation checked						
5. Polarity checked						
6. Switches checked						
7. Plug in working order						
8. Earth wire connected						
9. Wire to plug connection						
10. Equipment safe for use						

EQUIPMENT TYPE:	EQUIPMENT ID NO:	APPOINTED PERSON:	INSPECTION DATE:
INSPECTORS SIGNATURE:		INSPECTION DATE:	

COMPANY NAME/LOGO

SITE ADDRESS

Powered Mobile Plant Checklist for Contractors

QUESTION	EXPLANATION	COMMENT
1. Are operators properly trained and fit?	Workers operating certain types of powered mobile plant without direct supervision must hold appropriate certificates of competency. This includes the operation of slewing mobile cranes, non-slewing mobile, vehicle loading cranes, fork-lift trucks (except pedestrian-operated types), boom-type elevating work platforms, and truck-mounted concrete placing booms. Workers operating earthmoving plant such as front-end loaders, front-end loader/backhoes, skid steer loaders, excavators, dozers and draglines should have an appropriate qualification card or certificate. Insist that operators show you their certificates and qualifications, and record the details on the site register.	
2. Have operators been given training in the use of the particular machine?	Certificates of competency mean the operator has been assessed as generally competent to operate the classes of plant covered by the certificate. But it does not necessarily mean the operator is familiar with the particular make and model or the particular attachments being used with the plant. Make sure operators are familiar with their machine and attachments, that they have the operator's manual and that they understand the safe operating procedures for the work.	
3. Is plant properly maintained, checked and serviced?	Make sure plant is in a serviceable condition when it arrives on site. In the case of plant, which has been hired or leased, insist that the supplier provides you with a copy of the latest inspection and maintenance record. Make sure all the inspection and service checks recommended by the supplier are carried out at the recommended intervals during the time the plant remains on site. Keep records on any inspections and maintenance to plant carried out while the plant is under your management and control. Make sure plant found to be unserviceable is taken out of operation until it is repaired or replaced.	
4. Is plant fitted with reversing beepers?	Make sure all trucks, mobile cranes and other types of powered mobile plant are fitted with properly operating devices to warn people who are at risk from their movement. A combination of lights and reversing beeper is strongly recommended.	
5. Is plant fitted with ROPS and FOPS?	Tractors, rough terrain equipment or other powered mobile plant subject to the risk of overturning need a properly constructed and fitted roll-over protective structure (ROPS) to safeguard the operator from injury. Likewise, where there is any danger of falling debris, a suitable and robust falling objective protective structure (FOPS) is needed to protect the operator.	

QUESTION	EXPLANATION	COMMENT
6. Is plant being operated safely?	Check that plant is being operated in accordance with the supplier's recommendations and the operator's manual. Where, for any reason, the plant is to operate outside its normal conditions or in an abnormal environment, make sure that any additional hazard has been identified and any risk associated with this has been properly controlled.	
7. Are safety harnesses being used where necessary?	Boom-type elevating work platforms (cherry pickers, travel towers, boom lifts etc) should be supplied with a safety harness and lanyard for each person working in the basket. Make sure these are properly used at all times and are securely fixed to the proper anchorages within the basket. If the occupants of a basket are not safeguarded with a harness, a sudden failure of the knuckle joint at the end of the boom can throw them to their death.	
8. Is unattended plant properly secure?	Make sure plant is left in a properly stowed safe configuration whenever it is unattended. Loads should never be left suspended. Elevating work platforms and earthmoving plant should be fully lowered. Wherever possible, park plant overnight within the properly secured confines of the building site. Where this is not possible, make sure plant is secure against vandalism or joyriding. Where it is necessary to leave plant adjacent to public roads or pedestrian areas, make sure it is securely barricaded and, where appropriate, clearly marked with warning lamps.	
9. Are persons permitted to ride on vehicles?	Persons required to ride on construction vehicles must be provided with safe seating and any other protection that may be required.	
NAME:	SIGNATURE:	DATE:

COMPANY NAME/LOGO

SITE ADDRESS

Personal Protective Equipment Issue List for Contractors

NAME: CO. NO.:

CONDITIONS OF ISSUE

1. PPE will be issued at expense of the Company.
2. PPE remains the property of the Company and must be handed back on termination of service.
3. Loss or willful damage to PPE may result in disciplinary action being taken against the employee after an investigation.
4. I will immediately report if PPE issued to me is lost or damaged.
5. I will wear/use PPE issued to me where and whenever required to do so.
6. PPE may not be removed from the Company premises.
7. I understand that it is a legal requirement to wear PPE and that refusal to do so can lead to disciplinary procedures being instituted.
8. I have received comprehensive training on the use and limitations of PPE.

I understand and accept all the conditions of issue above.

SIGNATURE: **DATE:**

Overall	Cont. Suit Pants	Cont.Suit Top	Dust Coat	Apron	Hard Hat	Gum Boots	Safety Shoes	Gloves	Safety Goggles	Face Shield	Welding Hood
Self Cont. Respirator	**Respirator**	**Dust Mask**	**Hearing Protection**	**Safety Belt**	**Thermal Suit**	**Thermal Jacket**	**Jersey**	**Socks**	**FIRST AID KIT**		

NAME: SIGNATURE: DATE:

COMPANY NAME/LOGO

SITE ADDRESS

Personal Protective Equipment Requirement List for Contractors

SYMBOLIC SIGN	DESCRIPTION	QUANTITY	IF APPLICABLE MOTIVATE
	Overall		
	2 – Piece Suit Pants		
	2 – Piece Suit Top		
	Dust Coat		
	Apron		
	Hard Hat		
	Gum Boots		
	Safety Shoes		
	Gloves		
	Safety Glasses		
	Face Shield		
	Welding Hood		
	Breathing Apparatus		

SYMBOLIC SIGN	DESCRIPTION	QUANTITY	IF APPLICABLE MOTIVATE
	Respirator		
	Dust/Chemical Mask		
	Hearing Protection		
	Full Body Harness		
	Thermal Suit		
	Thermal Jacket		
	Jersey		
	Socks		
	Other Unspecified PPE Required		

NAME:	SIGNATURE:	DATE:

COMPANY NAME/LOGO

SITE ADDRESS

Public Safety Checklist for Contractors

QUESTION	EXPLANATION	COMMENT
1. Have you complied with local government requirements?	Local municipal councils may require you to take out certain permits and institute certain safeguards to properly protect adjoining property, roadways, footpaths and other public space. Check with the Council to make sure you have fully met local government requirements.	
2. Is the site secure?	Children and the general public need to be protected from wandering into danger on building sites. In populated areas, securely fence your site and lock it up when it is unattended.	
3. Is traffic movement properly managed?	Make sure entrances to the site for trucks and mobile plant are properly constructed. Make sure the public is in no danger from traffic movement to and from the site and from trucks loading and unloading alongside the site. Where necessary, post a flagman to safely direct passing traffic and pedestrians. Never allow cranes to load and unload trucks over passing traffic or pedestrians. In high-volume areas, you may need to construct temporary protective gantries or covered ways over walkways. You may also need properly constructed crane loading bays with swing-out gates and warning lights to separate passing traffic from crane-lifted loads.	
4. Is the public protected from dust and debris?	You may need to provide full-height perimeter scaffolds alongside building walls, which are in close proximity to public space. These may also need to be fully sheeted in shade cloth and/or fitted with protective fans to make sure debris is fully contained. Where necessary, fix hoardings around the base of scaffolds to prevent children from climbing them. You may need to regularly hose areas where work is creating excessive dust. Make sure that abrasive blasting, oxy-cutting and welding is done behind proper guards to prevent any injury to the public.	
5. Is work on public space being properly managed?	Where scaffolds or gantries need to be constructed over footpaths or laneways, organise for the work to be done at times where pedestrian traffic is least. Barricade the area under construction and provide alternative safe access past the work area. Similarly, barricade excavation areas and earth moving plant before any digging commences.	
NAME:	SIGNATURE:	DATE:

COMPANY NAME/LOGO

SITE ADDRESS

Roofing Checklist for Contractors

QUESTION	EXPLANATION	COMMENT
1. Is there safe access to roof areas?	Where there is no permanent access to roof areas, provide properly constructed temporary access. Portable industrial-grade ladders, secured against movement, pitched at about 75 degrees (1 in 4) and extending at least 900 mm above the stepping-off point, may be suitable for minor works. For major roofing work, provide a scaffold access tower, preferably one with temporary stairways. Where more than two workers are likely to access the roof at the same time, provide an access tower, which is at least medium duty. Provide a heavy-duty access tower where more than five workers are likely to be on the roof. Never allow workers to use elevating work platforms or barrow hoists to gain access to the roof.	
2. Have existing roofs been thoroughly checked?	Before commencing work on an existing roof, make sure it has been thoroughly inspected to determine its strength. Check the condition of roof trusses, rafters, purlins and roof battens. Identify all areas of fragile roofing such as cement sheeting and fibreglass skylights. Check the fixing and strength of safety mesh, paying particular attention to any signs of heavy corrosion. Strengthen any suspect areas of roof support with temporary props or similar.	
3. Are workers protected from falling off roof edges?	Falls from heights is the single most serious risk associated with roof work. Wherever there is any danger of a worker being killed or seriously injured by falling over the roof edge, provide an appropriate means of protection. Where a scaffold has been provided for construction of the walls or guttering, leave it in place until the roof work is complete. Where this is not possible, use a temporary guardrailing system. There are proprietary guardrailing systems available which are suitable for a wide range of roofing situations. For the rare occasions when guardrailing is not practicable, consider using safety line systems. Make sure that any safety line system is securely anchored and is set up so that inertia reel lines cannot be severed on sharp edges. Also make sure that the lines can be used without creating the "pendulum effect" in the event of a worker falling.	
4. Are workers protected from falling from incomplete roofs?	For metal deck roofing, the best way to protect roof workers from falling over leading edges is to cover the entire roof area with safety mesh before the roof is laid. This also provides ongoing protection for future roof maintenance and repair work. For roof tiling work, the close spacing of roof battens is usually adequate to safeguard workers from leading edge falls.	

QUESTION	EXPLANATION	COMMENT
5. Are workers protected from falling through skylights and penetrations?	Skylights which are not protected with safety mesh and penetrations left for the installation of airconditioning, etc, can be a danger to roof workers. Securely cover them or fix temporary guardrailing around them.	
6. Are people protected from the dangers of falling material?	Isolate the area below roof work wherever there is any danger of people being struck by falling material, debris or tools. Also isolate areas under roof edges unless toeboards are fixed to temporary guardrailing to contain all material, debris and loose tools.	
7. Are roof workers' tools and equipment being used safely?	Electrical leads and power tools should be protected by earth leakage and should be well maintained, fully serviceable and regularly inspected and tested. Use a tagging system, which records the date of the last test. Take particular care to ensure extension leads are not likely to be damaged by sharp edges.	
8. Do roof workers have appropriate footwear?	Roof workers need protective footwear that gives them a non-slip and flexible grip on the roof surface.	
NAME:	SIGNATURE:	DATE:

COMPANY NAME/LOGO

SITE ADDRESS

Site Establishment Checklist for Contractors

QUESTION	EXPLANATION	COMMENT
1. Is the site secure?	Once you have taken control of a building site in a populated area, secure it. Put a chain mesh fence or plywood hoarding at least 2.1metres high around your site with lockable gates. Lock up the site whenever it is unattended to prevent children or other people from wandering in to danger.	
2. Have you provided the right amenities for the workers?	Workers need clean and hygienic portable sheds or other suitably protected areas where they can change and store clothing, eat meals and take shelter from bad weather. Provide lunch rooms. Provide a ready supply of cool, clean drinking water. Make sure workers have easy access to clean and well maintained toilets and washing facilities.	
3. Are your first aid and emergency systems in place?	Have a sufficient number of qualified first aiders for the size of the job. Always have a first aider on site whenever work is occurring. Keep a well maintained first aid kit in a suitable location. Place a prominent Notice near your telephone which lists all the necessary emergency phone numbers, including ambulance, police, fire service and doctor. Make sure you have an emergency evacuation procedure and make sure all workers understand what they must do in the event of an accident or emergency. Prepare and post up clear directions to guide emergency services to your site.	
4. Have you checked existing grounds and buildings?	Check for the presence of asbestos before commencing work on existing buildings. Check for dangerous goods or hazardous substances stored in buildings, cellars or tanks. Check for soil contamination. Identify the locations of all underground services. Check for live electrical wiring. Check the condition and strength of roofs, floors, stairs, guardrailing, walls and structural members. Check that fire services are adequate and working. You may need to place additional extinguishers for the work.	
5. Have you posted the right signs and notices?	Where appropriate, the correct hazchem signs must be displayed at the gate where they can be easily seen by emergency services personnel. If it is a dangerous goods site, you will also need an up-to-date manifest in a locked container at or near the gate where it can be accessed by emergency services. You should have a prominent sign at the gate advising all visitors to report to the site office. Put up signs depicting the necessary types of personal protective equipment (such as safety helmets, hearing protection, safety glasses, breathing masks and safety footwear).	

QUESTION	EXPLANATION	COMMENT
6. Are the right registers and forms on site?	You must keep a register of injuries so that workers can record any workplace incident or injury. Make sure the workers know where it is and are encouraged to use i. Ensure that all other registers as required in terms of the Construction regulations are on site.	
7. Do you have a site induction program?	Make sure all workers have been properly informed of, and fully understand, your safety rules and site procedures. Keep a site induction record.	
8. Have your workers elected a health & safety representative?	Encourage your workers to elect one of their own as their health and safety representative. Send him or her to a training course for health and safety representatives as soon as practicable. Consult fully with the health and safety representatives at all stages of the job planning and encourage open and frank two-way communication and cooperation with your workers' health and safety representative.	
9. Have you identified your safety needs for the whole job?	Sit down with your workers and their health and safety representatives and go through all stages of the project so that the right safety systems and safety equipment requirements for each part of the work is recognised and understood and can be properly planned in advance of the work. All risks to health and safety must be eliminated from the work or, where this is not practicable, the risk must be controlled in the most effective ways to safeguard people from harm. Never rely on "common sense".	
NAME:	SIGNATURE:	DATE:

COMPANY NAME/LOGO

SITE ADDRESS

Trenching & Excavation Checklist for Contractors

QUESTION	EXPLANATION	COMMENT
1. Have all underground services been located?	Before digging starts, make sure you know the exact location of any underground electrical cables, gas lines, water and sewage and telecommunications cables. Do not rely solely on site plans and drawings as these are sometimes not accurate or complete. Seek assistance from the local services and distribution companies.	
2. Is earthmoving plant being used safely?	Check that plant operators are appropriately qualified and competent. Make sure all earthmoving plant is properly maintained and fully serviceable. Check that operators are not undermining existing buildings or temporary structures such as scaffolds and formwork. Make sure spoil is being kept at least half a meter back from the edge of trenches and that earthmoving plant is a safe distance from the edge of excavations. Make sure unattended front-end loaders, backhoes and excavators are always left with the bucket fully lowered to the ground. When parked overnight alongside roads or on other public space, make sure earthmoving plant is locked up and barricaded with warning lamps to alert traffic.	
3. Are workers protected from trench collapse?	Never allow workers to enter a trench or shaft which is greater than 1. meter deep unless it has been safely battered back, or it has been properly shored, or the workers are fully protected within a trench shield. Shoring should be positioned and fixed from above, never from below. All timber used in ground support should be at least F8 grade hardwood. Never use softwood because this can fail suddenly without warning, whereas hardwood will start to creak loudly when it is becoming overloaded, warning workers to leave the trench immediately. Make sure all workers in excavations always wear safety helmets.	
4. Are confined space precautions needed?	Where there is any possibility of a hazardous atmosphere within an excavation, the extra precautions for entry into confined spaces must be put in place.	
5. Are people safeguarded from falling into excavations?	Make sure trenches, shafts and excavations are properly barricaded, covered or isolated to prevent people falling into them. Whenever an excavation is to be left unattended, make sure it is secured to prevent children or other people from wandering into danger.	
6. Is there safe access to trenches and shafts?	Never allow workers to climb up and down the soldier sets used in trench shoring, because they can loosen or damage the support system, triggering a trench collapse. Make sure industrial-grade portable ladders are used to gain access to the excavation floor.	

QUESTION	EXPLANATION	COMMENT
7. Is someone else always present when a worker is below ground?	Never allow anyone to work alone in a trench or shaft. Make sure there is always another person close by who can provide help or get help if necessary.	
8. Are open excavations being regularly inspected?	The condition of soil surrounding trenches and shafts can change quickly due to the soil drying out, changes in the water table or water saturation of the soil. Make sure the soil condition and the state of shoring, battering and trenches walls is frequently checked for signs of earth fretting, slipping, slumping or ground swelling. Where necessary, repair the excavation or strengthen the shoring system from above before allowing work below ground to continue.	
NAME OF APPOINTED COMPETENT PERSON:	SIGNATURE:	DATE:

COMPANY NAME/LOGO

SITE ADDRESS

Trenching and Excavation Checklist for Contractors

SITE LOCATION:		
DATE:	TIME:	COMPETENT PERSON:
SOIL TYPE:		
SOIL CLASSIFICATION:	EXCAVATION DEPTH:	EXCAVATION WIDTH:
TYPE OF PROTECTIVE SYSTEM USED:		

Indicate for each item: YES – NO – or N/A for not applicable

1. General Inspection of Jobsite:

A.

Excavations, adjacent areas, and protective systems inspected by a competent person daily before the start of work.

B.

Competent person has the authority to remove employees from the excavation immediately.

C.

Surface encumbrances removed or supported.

D.

Employees protected from loose rock or soil that could pose a hazard by falling or rolling into the excavation.

E.

Hard hats worn by all employees.

F.

Spoils, materials, and equipment set back at least two feet from the edge of the excavation.

G.

Barriers provided at all remotely located excavations, wells, pits, shafts, etc.

H.

Walkways and bridges over excavations four feet or more in depth are equipped with standard guardrails and toeboards.

I.

Warning vests or other highly visible clothing provided and worn by all employees exposed to public vehicular traffic.

J.

Employees required to stand away from vehicles being loaded or unloaded.

K.

Warning system established and utilized when mobile equipment is operating near the edge of the excavation.

L.

Employees prohibited from going under suspended loads.

M.

Employees prohibited from working on the faces of slopes or benched excavations above other employees.

2. Utilities:

A.

Utility companies contacted and/or utilities located.

B.

Exact location of utilities marked.

C.

Underground installations protected, supported, or removed when excavation is open.

3. Means of Access and Egress:

A.

Lateral travel to means of egress no greater than 25 feet in excavations four feet or more in depth.

B.

Ladders used in excavations secured and extended three feet above the edge of the trench.

C.

Structural ramps used by employees designed by a competent person.

D.

Structural ramps used for equipment designed by a registered professional engineer (RPE).

E.

Ramps constructed of materials of uniform thickness, cleated together on the bottom, equipped with no-slip surface.

F.

Employees protected from cave-ins when entering or exiting the excavation.

4. Wet Conditions:

A.

Precautions take to protect employees from the accumulation of water.

B.

Water removal equipment monitored by a competent person.

C.

Surface water or runoff diverted or controlled to prevent accumulation in the excavation.

D.

Inspections made after every rainstorm or other hazard-increasing occurrence.

5. Hazardous Atmosphere:

A.

Atmosphere within the excavation tested where there is a reasonable possibility of an oxygen deficiency, combustible or other harmful contaminant exposing employees to a hazard.

B.

Adequate precautions taken to protect employees from exposure to an atmosphere containing less than 19.5% oxygen and/or to other hazardous atmospheres.

C.

Ventilation provided to prevent employee exposure to an atmosphere containing flammable gas in excess of 10% of the lower explosive limit of the gas.

D.

Testing conducted often to ensure that the atmosphere remains safe.

E.

Emergency equipment, such as breathing apparatus, safety harness and lifeline, and/or basket stretcher readily available where hazardous atmospheres could or do exist.

F.

Employees trained to use personal protective and other rescue equipment.

G.

Safety harness and lifeline used and individually attended when entering bell bottom or other deep confined excavations.

6. Support Systems:

A.

Materials and/or equipment for support systems selected based on soil analysis, trench depth, and expected loads.

B.

Materials and equipment used for protective systems inspected and in good condition.

C.

Materials and equipment not in good condition have been removed from service.

D.

Damaged materials and equipment used for protective systems inspected by a registered professional engineer (RPE) after repairs and before being placed back into service.

E.

Protective systems installed without exposing employees to the hazards of cave-ins, collapses, or threat of being struck by materials or equipment.

F.

Members of support system securely fastened to prevent failure.

G.

Support systems provided in ensure stability of adjacent structures, buildings, roadways, sidewalks, walls, etc.

H.

Excavations below the level of the base or footing supported, approved by an RPE.

I.

Removal of support systems progresses from the bottom and members are released slowly as to note any indication of possible failure.

J.

Backfilling progresses with removal of support system.

K.

Excavation of material to a level no greater than two feet below the bottom of the support system and only if the system is designed to support the loads calculated for the full depth.

L.

Shield system placed to prevent lateral movement.

M.

Employees are prohibited from remaining in shield system during vertical movement.

CORRECTIVE ACTIONS AND REMARKS:

Daily Trenching Log

DAILY TRENCHING LOG

DATE:
SIGNATURE:

WEATHER:
PROJECT:

Was One Call System contacted:
Yes_______
No_______

Protective system: Trench shield (box)
Trench shield (box)__________
Wood Shoring__________

Sloping__________
Other__________

Purpose of trenching: Drainage
Drainage__________
Water__________

Sewer__________
Gas__________

Other__________

Were visual soil tests made:
Yes_______
No_______

If yes, what type?

Were manual soil tests made:
Yes_______
No_______

If yes, what type?

Type of soil:
Stable Rock_______
Type A _______
Type B _______
Type C _______

Surface encumbrances:
Yes_______
No_______

If yes, what type?

Water conditions:
Wet_______
Dry_______
Submerged _______

Hazardous atmosphere exists:
Yes_______
No_______

(If yes, follow confined space entry procedures policy; complete Confined Space Entry Permit; monitor for toxic gas(es))

Is trenching or excavation exposed to public vehicular traffic (exhaust emission):
Yes_______ No_______

(If yes, refer to confined space entry procedures; complete Confined Space Entry Permit; monitor for toxic gas(Es))

Measurements of trench:
Depth_______
Length_______
Width _______

Is ladder within 25 feet of all workers:
Yes_______
No_______

Is excavated material stored two feet or more from edge of excavation:
Yes_______
No_______

Are employees exposed to public vehicular traffic:
Yes _______
No_______

(If yes, warning vests required)

Are other utilities protected:
Yes_______
No_______

(Water, sewer, gas or other structures)

Are sewer or natural gas lines exposed:

Yes________

No________

(If yes, refer to confined space entry procedures policy; complete Confined Space Entry Permit; monitor for toxic gas(Es))

Periodic inspection:

Yes________

No________

Did employees receive training in excavating:

Yes________

No________

ANNEXURE E

PERMITS

COMPANY NAME/LOGO

SITE ADDRESS

CONFINED SPACE ENTRY PERMIT

Date and Time Issued:	Date and Time Expires:
Job site/Space I.D.:	Job Supervisor:
Equipment to be worked on:	Work to be performed:

Stand-by personnel:
1. 2. 3. 4.

1. Atmospheric Checks: Time	Oxygen	%
	Explosive	% L.F.L.
	Toxic	PPM
2. Tester's signature:		

	N/A	YES	NO
3. Source isolation (No Entry): Pumps or lines blinded, disconnected, or blocked)			

	N/A	YES	NO
4. Ventilation Modification: Mechanical Natural Ventilation only			

5. Atmospheric check after isolation and Ventilation:	Oxygen % > 19.5 % Explosive % L.F.L < 10 % Toxic PPM < 10 PPM H(2)S
Time:	Testers signature:

6. Communication procedures:

7. Rescue procedures:

	YES	NO
8. Entry, standby, and back up persons: successfully completed required training? Is it current?		

	N/A	YES	NO
9. Equipment			
Direct reading gas monitor – tested			
Safety harnesses and lifelinesfor entry and standby persons			
Hoisting equipment			
Powered communications			
SCBA's for entry and standby persons			
Protective Clothing			
All electric equipment listed Class I, Division I, Group D and Non-sparking tools			

10. Periodic atmospheric tests:		
	Oxygen %	Time:
	Oxygen %	Time:
	Oxygen %	Time:
	Oxygen %	Time:
	Explosive %	Time:
	Explosive %	Time:
	Explosive %	Time:
	Explosive %	Time:
	Toxic %	Time:
	Toxic %	Time:
	Toxic %	Time:
	Toxic %	Time:

We have reviewed the work authorized by this permit and the information contained here-in. Written instructions and safety procedures have been received and are understood. Entry cannot be approved if any squares are marked in the "No" column. This permit is not valid unless all appropriate items are completed.

Permit Prepared By: (Supervisor):	Approved By: (Unit Supervisor):	Reviewed By (Cs Operations Personnel) :

This permit to be kept at job site. Return job site copy to Safety Office following job completion.

Copies: Safety Office
Unit Supervisor
Job site

COMPANY NAME/LOGO

SITE ADDRESS

HOT WORK PERMIT

GENERAL INFORMATION

Permit No.

Worksite Identification:.. Hot work to be Performed:..
....
Location/Building: .... Authorized Duration of Permit: Date: .... to ....
Time:...................... to...............

SOURCE OF IGNITION

- ☐ Acetylene torch
- ☐ Abrasive saw
- ☐ Electric arc
- ☐ Electric tools
- ☐ Heliarc welding
- ☐ Propane Torch
- ☐ Soldering
- ☐ Drilling
- ☐ Other

SOURCE OF IGNITION

THIS HOT WORK PERMIT MAY BE SIGNED AND HOT WORK AUTHORIZED ONLY AFTER SATISFACTORY COMPLIANCE WITH ALL ITEMS

- ☐ Floors swept clean of combustibles
- ☐ Remaining combustible or flammable materials 10 m horizontally as well as vertically from source of heat?
- ☐ Non-movable combustible or flammable materials isolated, covered/shielded with fire retardant material?
- ☐ Vertical and horizontal openings within 10 m sealed or covered for spark or vapour control?
- ☐ Heat transmission, conduction, radiation, controlled?
- ☐ Hazardous material transfers disconnected within 21 m of hot work?
- ☐ Lockout/tagout of electrical, mechanical, chemical, blanking, cap piping implemented?
- ☐ Vessels, equipment drained, purged, ventilated, cleaned?
- ☐ Inert gas blanket required?
- ☐ Welding, cutting fume ventilation or respirator required?
- ☐ Building/area air currents and outdoor wind direction known?
- ☐ Hazardous material spill location equipment and countermeasures available?
- ☐ Supervisor notified work location and time of operation?
- ☐ Involved personnel and contractor employees notified of hazards?
- ☐ Means of egress identified and available?
- ☐ Fire protection equipment available and operational?
- ☐ Automatic fire sprinkler system operational?
- ☐ Oxygen – rich environment evaluated?
- ☐ Continuous monitoring of atmospheric conditions maintained?
- ☐ Checking for flammable / combustible gas and oxygen levels?
- ☐ Special danger, caution, warning signs posted?
- ☐ Trenches over 1.5 m deep shored or sloped?
- ☐ Fire watch provided during work and 30 minutes after completion of work?
- ☐ Work areas and adjacent areas where sparks may have spread checked out 30 minutes after work completed?

APPROVALS AND AUTHORIZATIONS

This permit is valid as long as work conditions existing at the time of issuance continue. It expires on any change of condition that adversely affects safety of the work area while work is in progress.

STOP WORK IMMEDIATELY IF PLANT EMERGENCY ALARM SIGNALS AN EMERGENCY IN OR NEAR YOUR WORK AREA. FOLLOW FIRE WATCH INSTRUCTIONS.

I have personally inspected the location where the above work is to be done. I have checked for compliance with the safety precautions listed on the permit and authorized the work to be performed.

Title	Printed Name	Signature	Date
Originator/Approver			
Safety Officer			
Welder			
Fire Watch			

THIS PERMIT MUST BE POSTED ON JOB SITE. GOOD ONLY ON INDICATED DATE

COMPANY NAME/LOGO

SITE ADDRESS

SAFE WORK PERMIT

A copy of the SAFE WORK PERMIT must be kept at the work site at all times.

I ______________________, am required to carry out the work detailed below and request a permit to cover the following hazards, from the competent/responsible person, to access the following Plant/Apparatus/Area. (Indicate with an X which hazards are applicable)	CONFINED SPACE ENTRY	
	EXCAVATION	
Area/Machine/Equipment where work is to be carried out:	HAZARDOUS SUBSTANCE	
Description of work to be carried out:	HOT WORK	
	INCIDENTAL STARTING	
Names of persons who will be involved with the work: 1. __________________ 2. __________________ 3. __________________ 4.	ROOF WORK	
	SCAFFOLD	

DATE AND TIME OF COMMENCEMENT	**DATE:**	**TIME:**
ESTIMATED DATE AND TIME OF COMPLETION	**DATE:**	**TIME:**

HEALTH AND SAFETY PRECAUTIONS IDENTIFIED	CONFINED SPACE ENTRY	EXCAVATION	HAZARDOUS SUBSTANCE	ACCIDENTAL STARTING (LOCKING OUT)	ROOF WORK OR (SCAFFOLD)	HOT WORK
1. Specific hazards identified during site inspection.						
2. All flammable, combustible, toxic, corrosive materials and vapors have been removed.						
3. Protective equipment is available and serviceable.						
4. Trained, responsible person(s) posted as fire-watch with suitable fire extinguishers or confined space hazard observers.						
5. Permit holder and helpers/assistants have been instructed what to do in case of a fire/gassing/ substance exposure/collapsed excavation/ collapsed roof sheeting, etc.						

HEALTH AND SAFETY PRECAUTIONS IDENTIFIED	CONFINED SPACE ENTRY	EXCAVATION	HAZARDOUS SUBSTANCE	ACCIDENTAL STARTING (LOCKING OUT)	ROOF WORK OR (SCAFFOLD)	HOT WORK
6. The area/space is adequately ventilated.						
7. Valves and pipes leading to the work area/ confined space; switches/isolators or actuating levers have been closed and locked out/blanking off flanges in place.						
8. Suitable low voltage lighting available.						
9. From site inspection it would appear that the job could be safely performed.						
10. Personal gas monitor to be used.						
11. Other provisions made:						

WE ARE SATISFIED THAT THE ABOVE PRECAUTIONS HAVE BEEN TAKEN AND THAT IT SHOULD BE SAFE TO CARRY OUTTHE ABOVE MENTIONED WORK

COMPETENT/RESPONSIBLE PERSON	**NAME:**	**SIGNATURE:**	**DATE:**
PERMIT HOLDER	**NAME:**	**SIGNATURE:**	**DATE:**

WE CERTIFY THAT THE ABOVE JOB HAS BEEN COMPLETED, THE AREA WAS INSPECTED FOR ANY REMAINING.HAZARD OR CONDITION (e.g. fire) AND HAS BEEN CLEARED AND IS IN A SAFE CONDITION

COMPETENT/RESPONSIBLE PERSON	**SIGNATURE:**	**TIME:**	**DATE:**
PERMIT HOLDER	**SIGNATURE:**	**TIME:**	**DATE:**